Views from My Car
Flowers

Written by and Photographed by
Amy Dee Hosp

Views from My Car
Flowers

Written by and Photographed by
Amy Dee Hosp

The Liberty of It All
With Genes That Don't Fit ©

Copyright © 2019

ISBN: 9781706254539

All photographs and Art are copyrighted. Amy Hosp (The Liberty of It All) - All rights reserved. Photographs may not be reproduced and/or used publicly in any way without permission.
For questions you can e-mail me
Amy Hosp at hospamy@yahoo.com.

If you would like to purchase a print of any of the photos in the book go to
https://amy-hosp.pixels.com/

Other books by Amy Hosp:

Ehlers Danlos Syndrome with Liberty the Dog

Collection of Sketches For
Reaching Out to the Hurting and Lost

Whether it is a field of flowers, flowers standing all alone, flowers for decorating, or simply weeds, it's hard to look at them and not thank God for giving us such beauty to dance in our eyes.

Dear Reader,

Have you ever been able to dive into something that you are completely passionate about? I think we all try now and again to do this, but rarely do we really find the time to give it our best. There are so many things that I am passionate about, too many to ever get them all done, but I have jumped in with both feet and legs and arms, well let's just say that I am all in with one of them. If you are reading this right now, I bet you could guess that one of my passions is photography. Photography started for me as a hobby when I lived in Nigeria as a missionary. Of course, there were so many opportunities to capture my surroundings on film and I loved being able to look back at the pictures so I just fell in love with seizing what I knew I would want to share with everyone at home. Being able to put on film what I see around me reminds me of the Creator, God, who gave us this world to enjoy.

Most people recognize me as being reasonably resourceful and I guess I really am when resourcefulness is needed. My need for being resourceful is due to a couple rare genetic disorders that I was diagnosed with in 2012 and 2017.

    These disorders are called Ehlers Danlos Syndrome Classical type 1 and Osteogenesis Imperfecta type 1. These disorders can be very debilitating at times, more times than not for me, so in order to accomplish things I'm forced to think outside of the box. I've had to do this for so long I guess that has trained me to be a resourceful thinker.
    How is this related to photography? Most people who are photographers can walk around anywhere they need to so they can capture that picture they are hunting for. That's almost a requirement to get decent pictures. I don't have the ability to jump out of my car and walk long distances to get "that shot" so I had to come up with another plan. I do have a power wheelchair that I use at times, but that still doesn't allow me the ability I need to have good photos to enjoy and share with others. Since I love taking photos so much, I just kept snapping pictures right from inside of my car and as a result I have found a way to put my passion into action.
    My friends and I are always looking for something interesting to do together that usually involves getting out of town.

Not the getting out of town that takes you on an airplane, but rather just out to the country away from the city for and afternoon. One day we did just that. We were planning our day and deciding which direction we were going to travel in, north, south, east, or west and so we came to the conclusion that south was the way to go. We each had our refreshments, and music, a topic on our mind to discuss and a camera. These are truly no pressure no rush trips that we make but during this one trip we ran into a little problem. It was a fork in the road. Not the kind of fork needed for a piece of cake, but a fork in the road that you had to go either left or right or back the way you just came. We set there in the car for a minute each undecided about which way to go and someone in the car, most likely my silly self, said, "I saw a dead coon back behind us and his head was pointing right, I think he was telling us to go right." So, we did, until we saw another dead animal on the side of the road, you know, what most people call roadkill. When we saw that poor dead animal, roadkill, we paid close attention to which way its head was pointing because our short little escapade thus far that the dead coon had sent us on was very pleasant and we even found several interesting things to take photos of.

We knew if it weren't for that coon sacrificing his life for us that we would have never seen those interesting things. It was on that trip that a long-standing tradition of taking Roadkill Trips with our friends was born.

Ok, you are either laughing right now or wondering what in the world have I gotten myself into with this seemingly nice book of photos. Hold on, you'll understand in a minute, just keep swimming, oh, I mean reading. The rule is no matter which way the roadkill's head is pointing we must turn at the next available road in that direction. If it's pointing straight, we go straight. Rarely will we turn around if it's pointing where we have just traveled so we wait until we see another pointing roadkill head. We have found ourselves in some of the most beautiful amazing places with some of the best discoveries, including fun and yummy places to eat or get a snack.

We usually go out about three hours or so and then we challenge ourselves to get home without using a map or GPS. I don't remember ever getting so lost that we needed help but I'm not going to brag about that either because when I do that will be the day that we start getting lost.

These trips are so much fun, and I get the best photos because they are unplanned and I just snap shots of things that interest me, that within itself, is relaxing. So, how do my disorders that I have play into this? There have been numerous opportunities to jump out of the car and take photos, but I found that the more I did that the worse I would feel by the end of the day and then I would get cranky. Who wants to ride around on a Roadkill Trip with a cranky gal? No one that I know so I had to come up with a plan. My plan was to take the photos of our discoveries from my car window. yes, you heard me right, they are taken from either my car window or from the moon roof. Snapping photos this way helped me stay "nice" for the whole trip. I also saw that taking photos from inside the car as a challenge. I love taking photos from my car window. Now, not only are Roadkill Trips my thing, but Views from My Car are my thing. I have combined those two together to publish my photos to share with the world. I have too many photos to count so I have many categories to choose from to share. My photo book series is called Views from My Car: Flowers (or whatever the photos are that I'm sharing). I have maybe 5-10 outdoor photos that I took outside of my car like a normal person would but the rest of the outdoor pictures are all taken from inside of my car. Since I'm not able to get out of my car easily I've learned to look around me carefully to see what would make a nice photo. I have discovered that I can get photos of things and places that getting out of the car would be too dangerous to do, like standing on the side of a highway, or such.

    Here's to hoping that no one starts calling me the Roadkill Trip lady that looks for dead animals from her car, even though I do have a few very curious snapshots of some roadkill. I don't share those with too many people, and I may or may not publish a book about that one day. I do hope to be known as the resourceful lady with a camera that inspired you to chase your passion so that you may be blessed by the joy it brings you.

                                        Love, Amy

Shadows of A Ride

Road trips are so much fun but seeing your road tip play out like a movie by the reflection of the shadow of your car makes it much more interesting. Keep people guessing all the time by being yourself and driving out of the shadows.

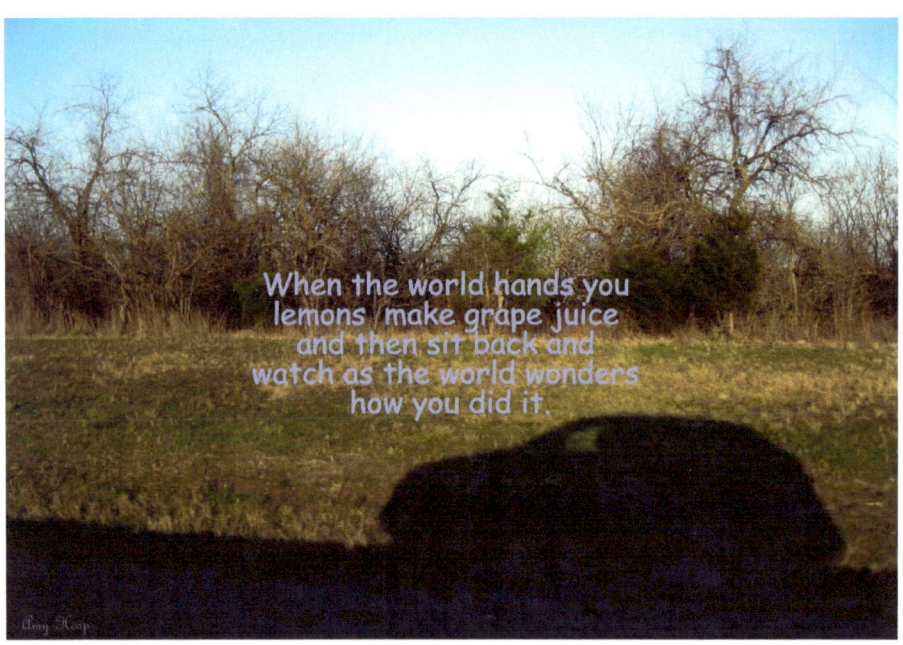

When the world hands you lemons, make grape juice and then sit back and watch as the world wonders how you did it.

Wildflower Love

Like a wildflower your love is beautiful and free
Your love not restricted by all the
rules that I set for me
Like a wildflower I find in the beauty of your
love freedom to explore and to grow
To become more of who I hoped to be as I feel
your love towards me flow
Like a wildflower your beauty
is in the spirit of your being
Created in a special way without us even seeing
Like a wildflower you were created for a purpose
beyond what we may never understand
And the beauty that I see in you reminds me
of the grace of God's hand
Like a wildflower growing wildly displaying
beautiful splashes of color special for our eyes
Your love has opened my heart and with grace
you have listened to my cries
Like a wildflower you love is beautiful and free
I thank God every day that He
sent you to love me.
Amy Hosp © 2019

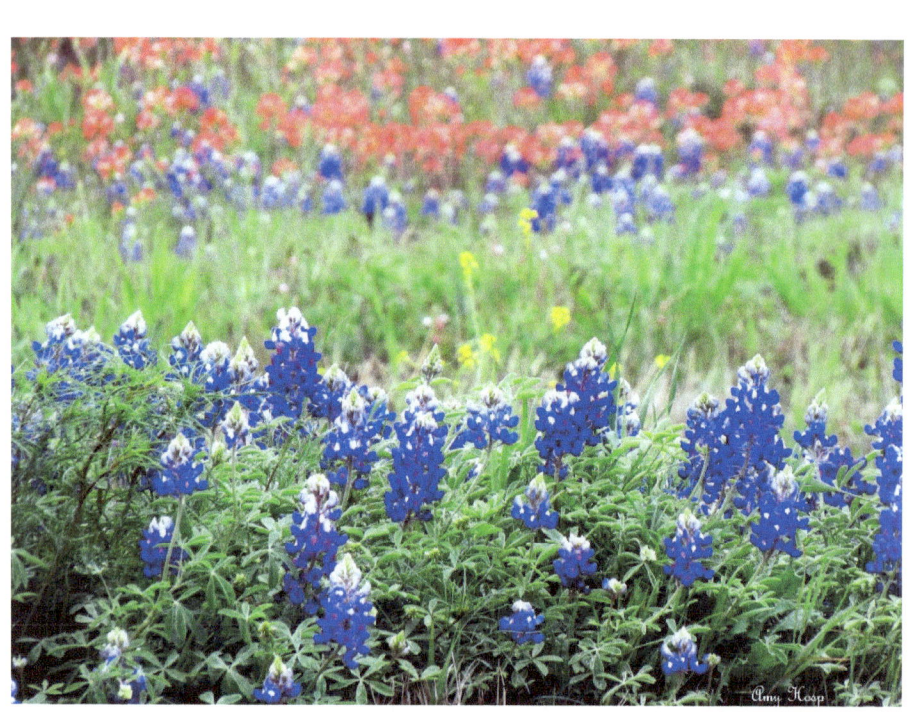

Bluebonnets are one of the best gifts that springtime gives us.

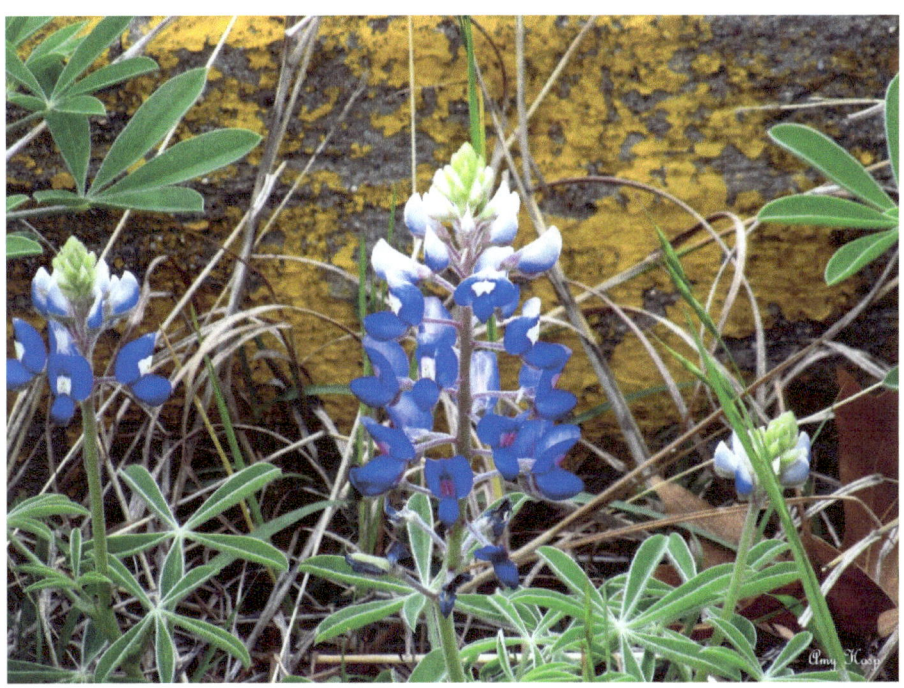

The bright rich colors of the Texas Bluebonnets are an ever reminder of the warmer weather that is on its way.

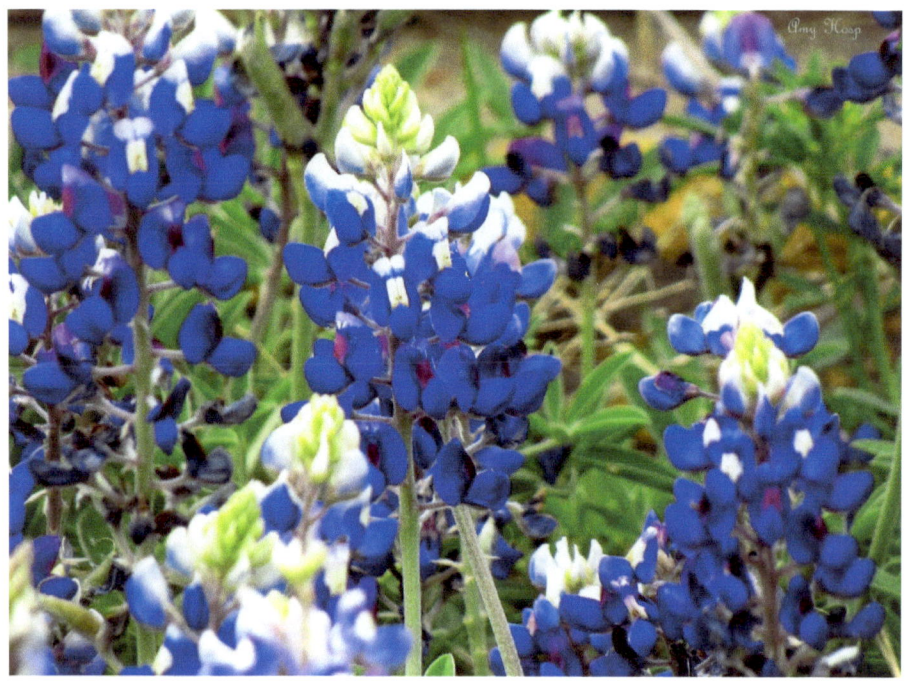

The Earth looks happy dressed in flowers.

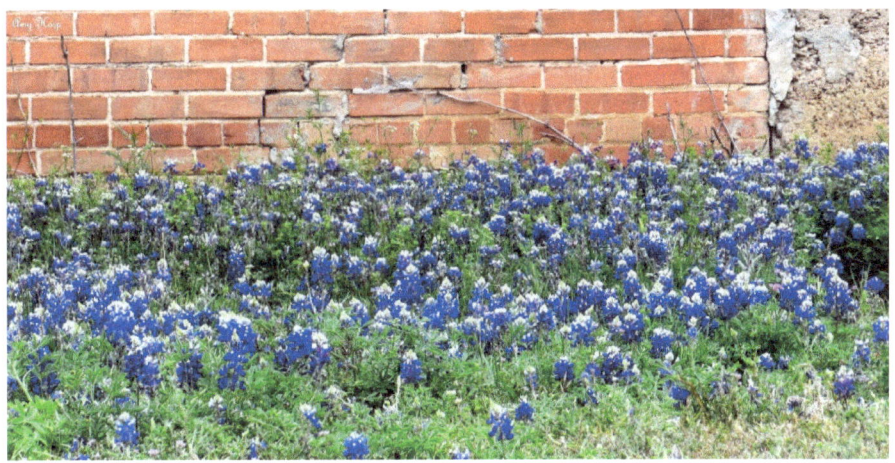

Children getting pictures taken while sitting among bluebonnets is a springtime rite of passage.

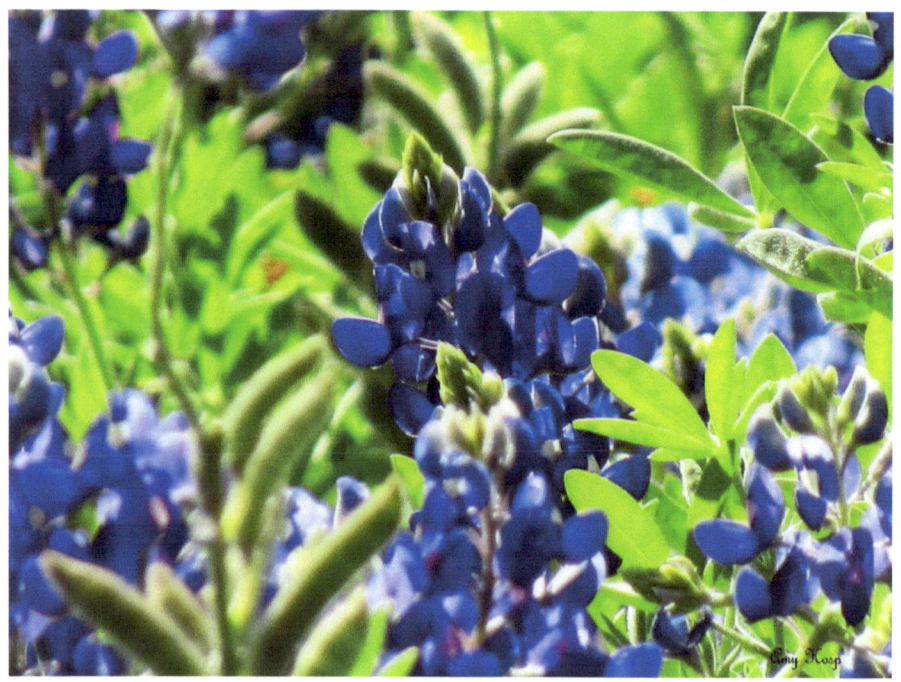

Bluebonnets are an ancient ancestor that reminds us from where we come. If you grew up going to school in Texas, then you studied about the Bluebonnets and heard the old Native American stories about how they came to be.

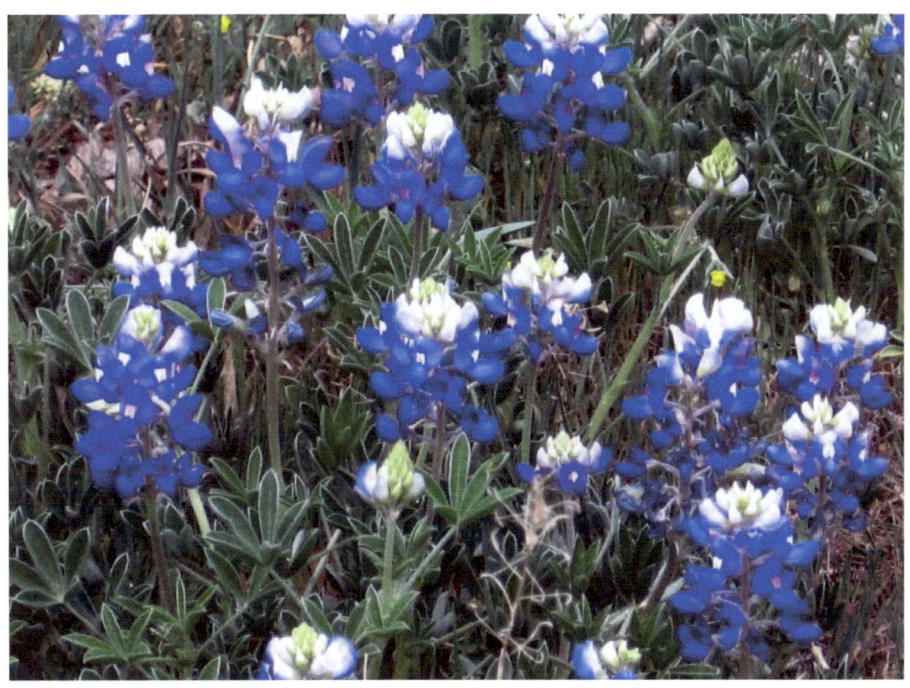

Heavy rains bring out the lily with its fragrant beauty.

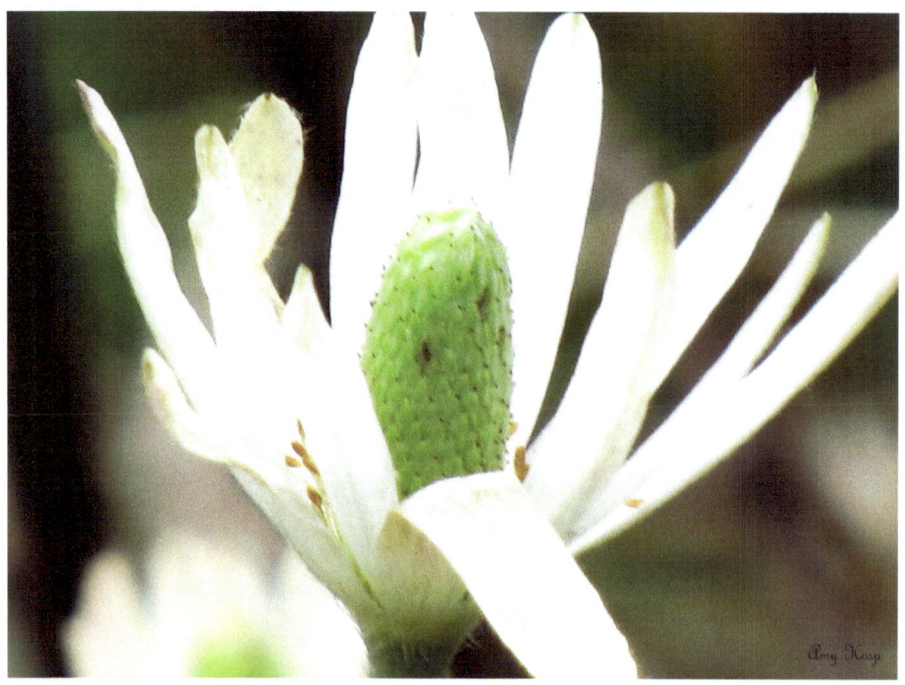

The Bible tells us in Mathew 6:28-29 that we are to consider the lilies of the field and look how they grow. They don't work or make their clothes. Solomon, being the richest man was not ever dressed as beautifully or stunningly as even one of the lilies.

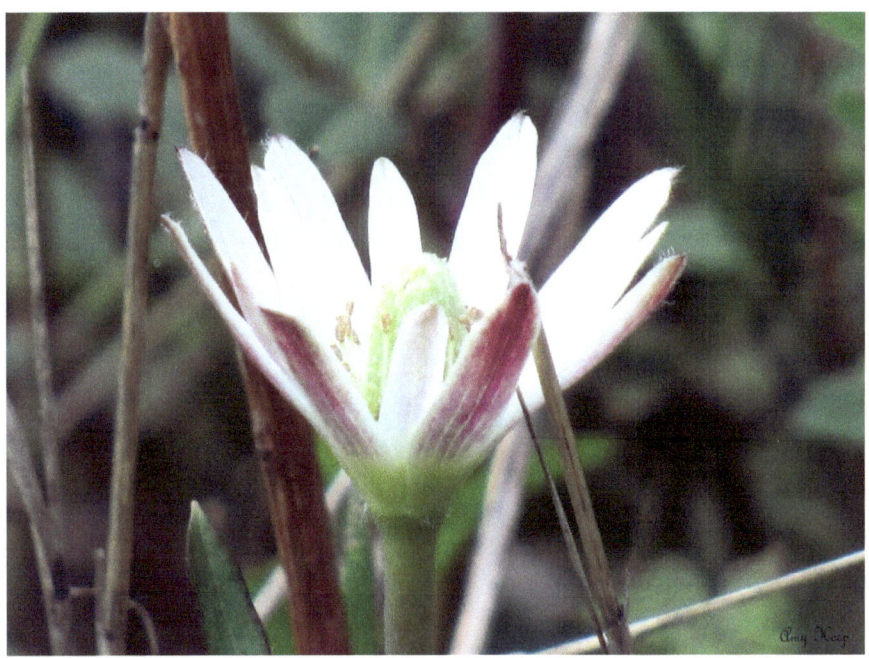

Sunflowers stand tall and sure, like a guard protecting its treasure.

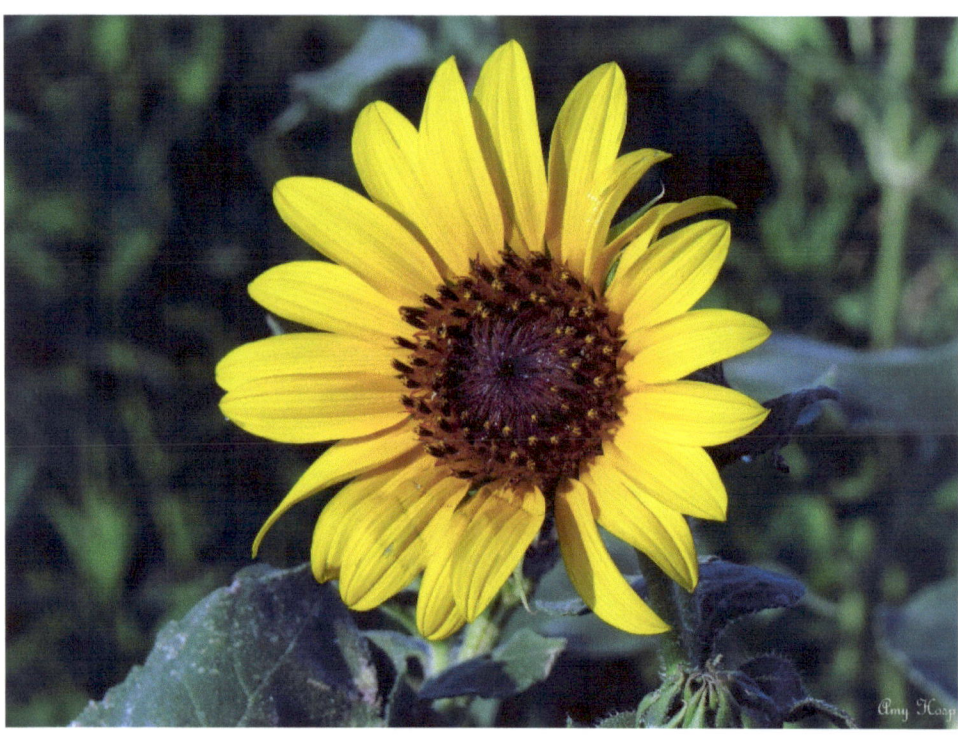

The sunflower is a consistent sign of growing crops and the hard work of the local farmers.

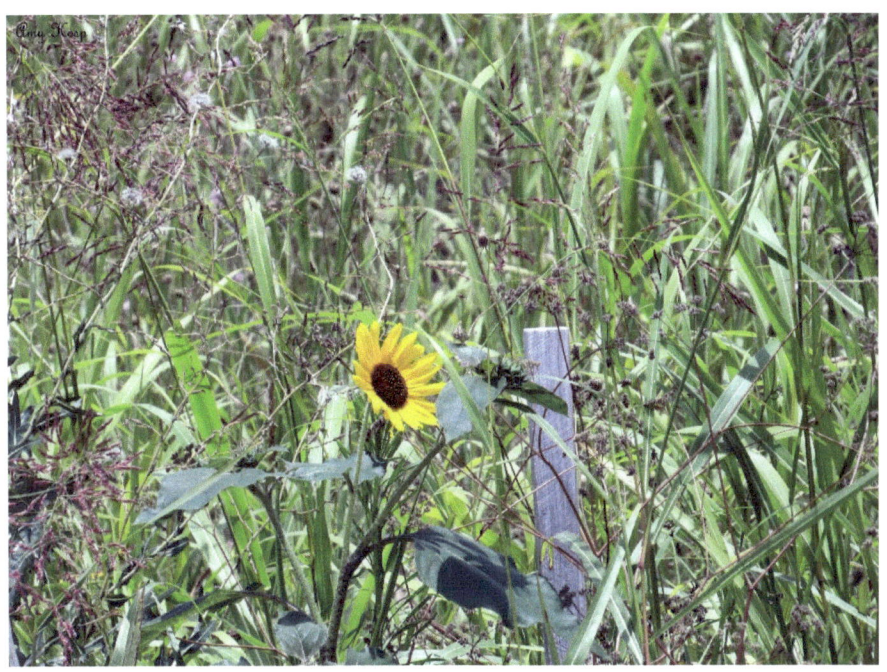

Sunflowers do not have the delicate tenderness that some flowers have, some people have bad members of clearing sunflowers from the fields, according to my mother who has that memory, and others celebrate these giants as a symbol of being with family drinking sweet tea on the back porch.

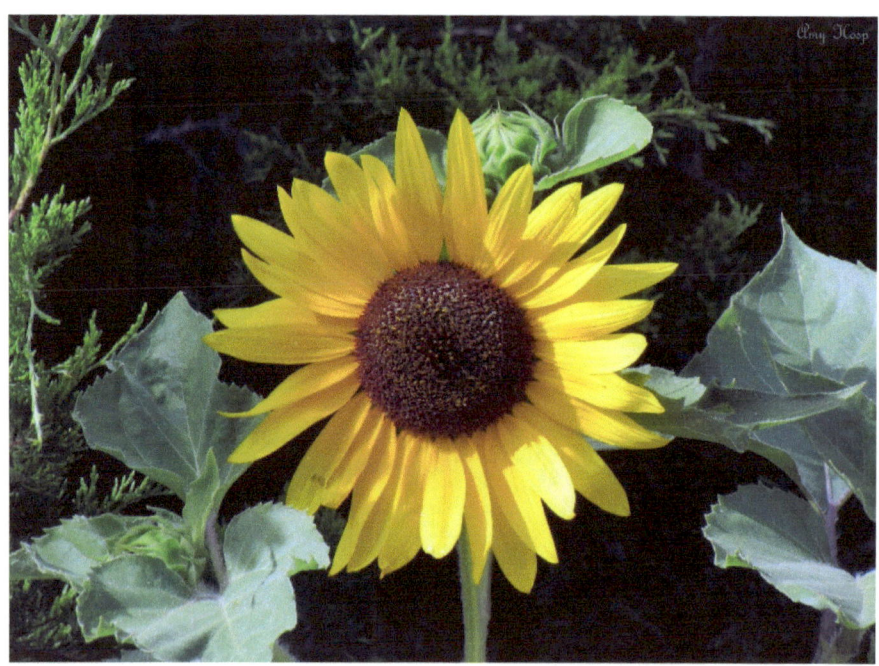

Abraham Lincoln said about flowers that we can complain about the roses because they have thorns, or that we can be glad that the thorns have roses. It's true that we often create the good and the bad with how we view things.

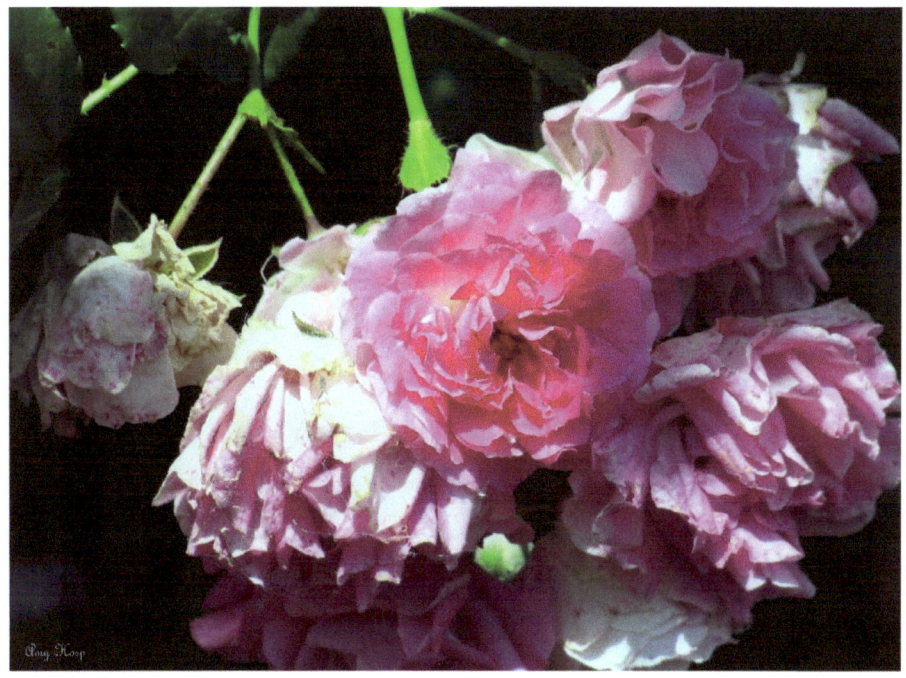

The iris carries the old fashion name of paper roses. The edges of the iris when curled, look like a colored piece of paper that is too delicate and fragile to touch.

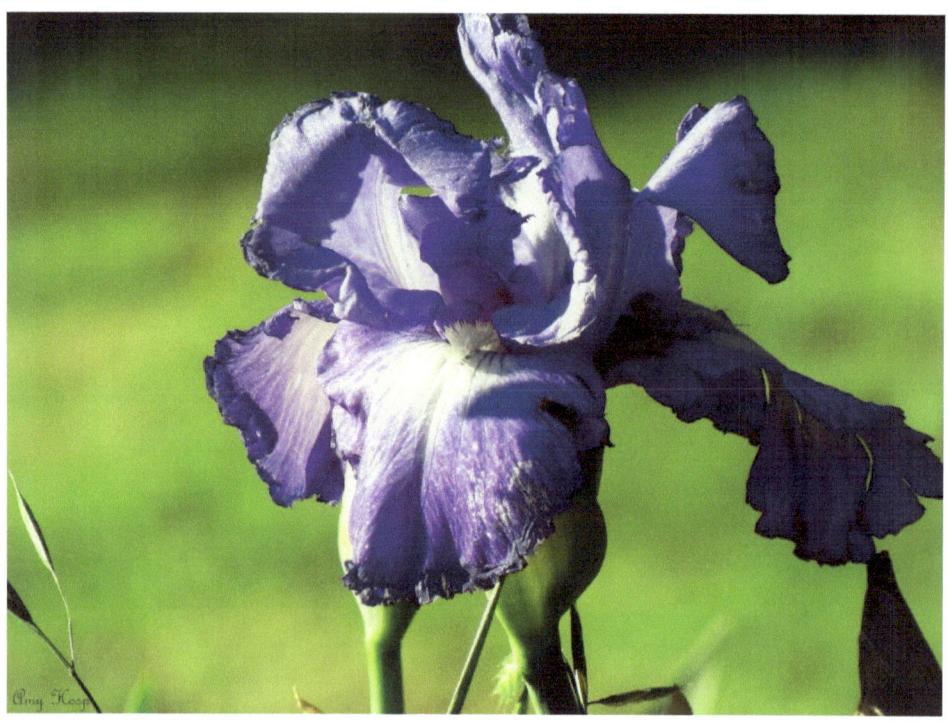

This iris reminds me or a dancer expressing her freedom to dance.

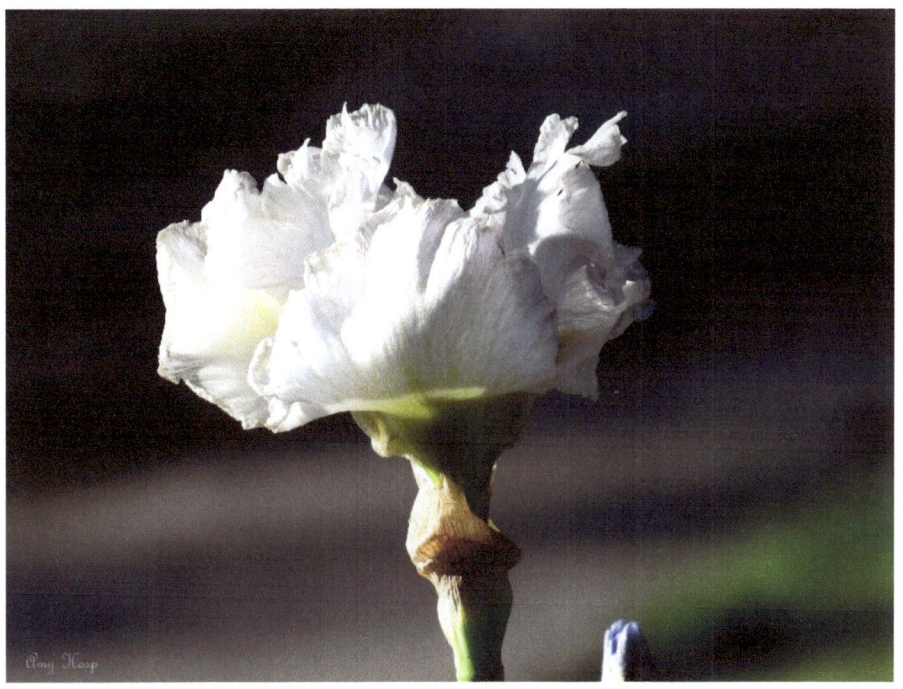

Martha Washington said that the greatest part of our happiness is not from our circumstances but on how we view them. This big beautiful hibiscus reminds me that if I will just look for it, God's beauty around me is far bigger than my troubles that I see before me.

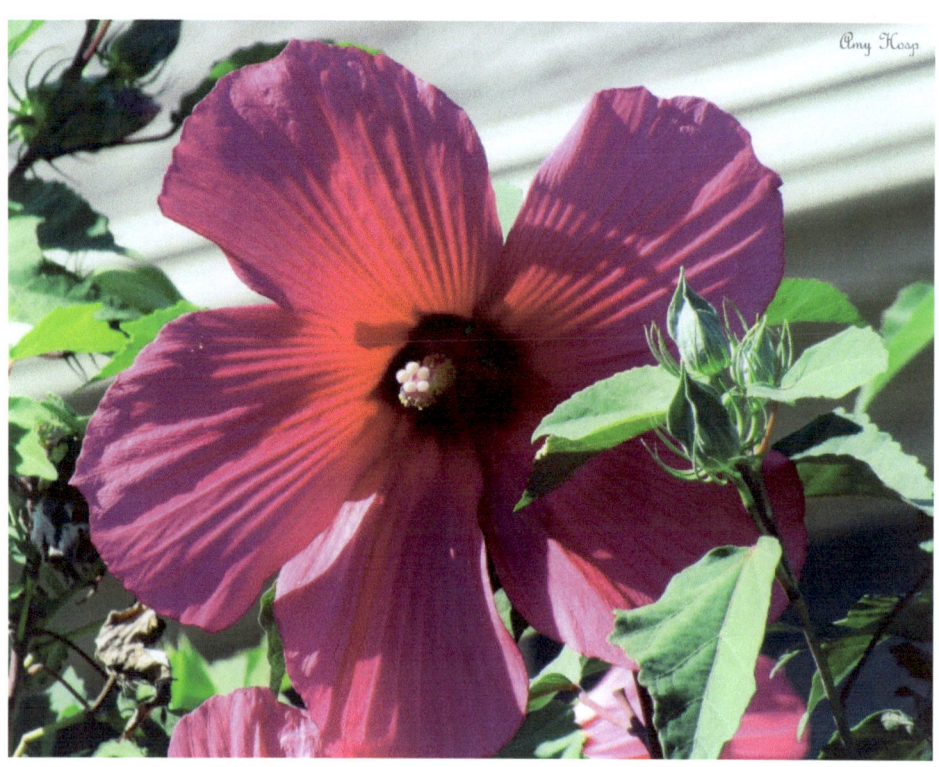

How can a weed produce such a silky shinny beauty like this? It's a reminder to me that even among the stickiness of life, beauty abounds.

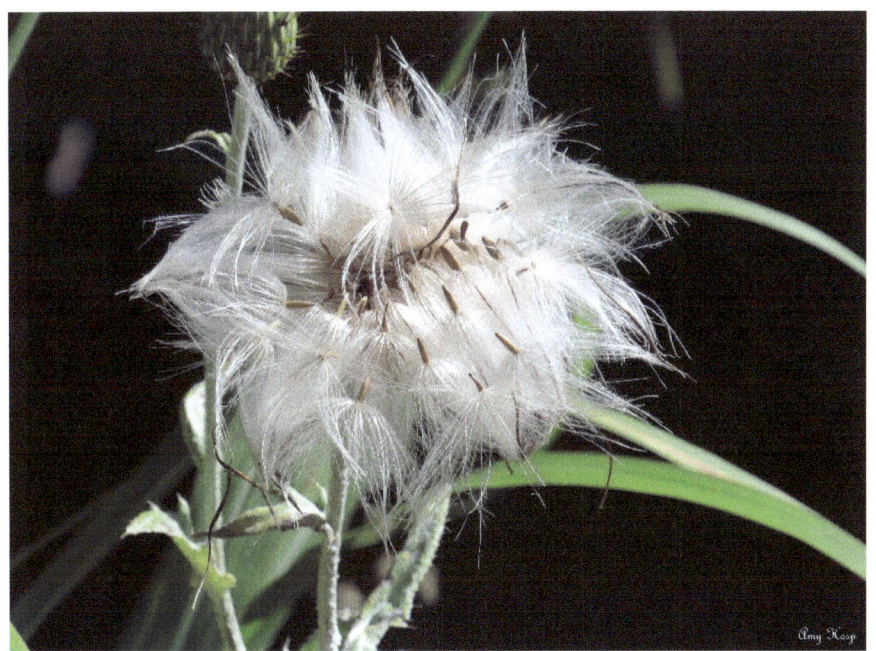

The prairies of North Central Texas are vast and beautiful. It's in these prairies that you can find beauty among the harshness.

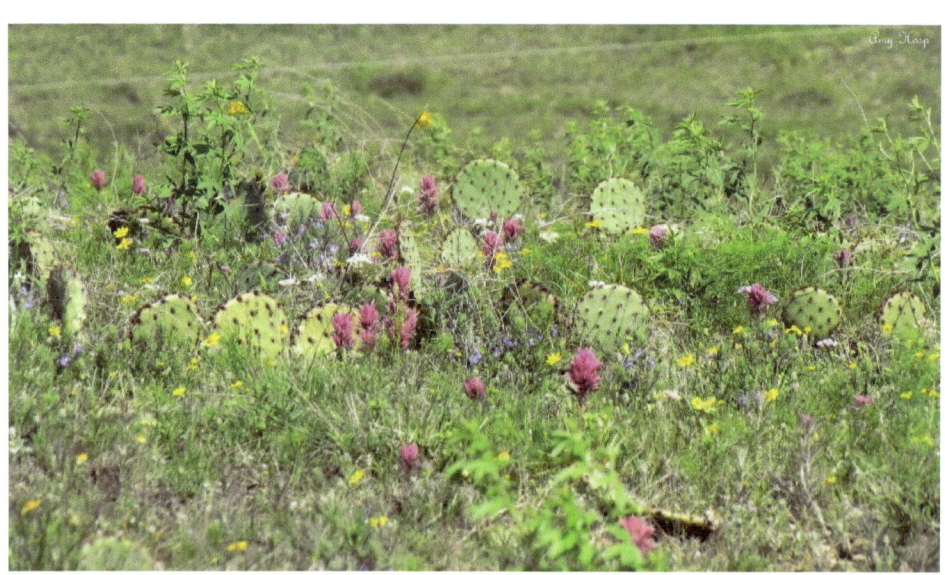

The colors of green, pink, yellow and purple in this prairie are some of my favorite. I feel ever peaceful seeing the combination of the different colors and textures melding together to offer such a beautiful sight.

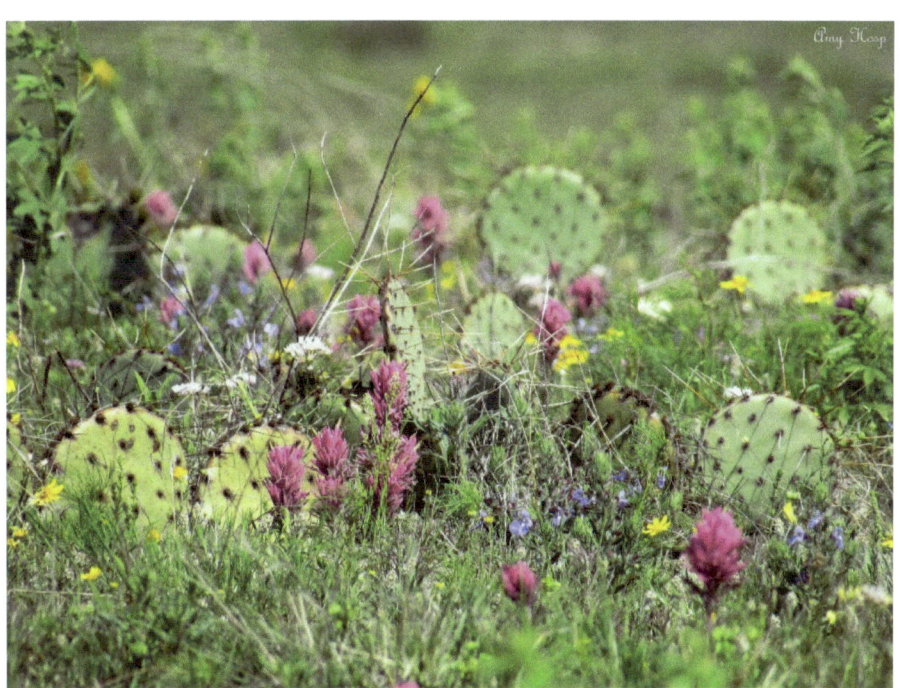

Having an afternoon drive across the countryside away from the business of the city refreshes the soul like no other activity that
I treat myself with.

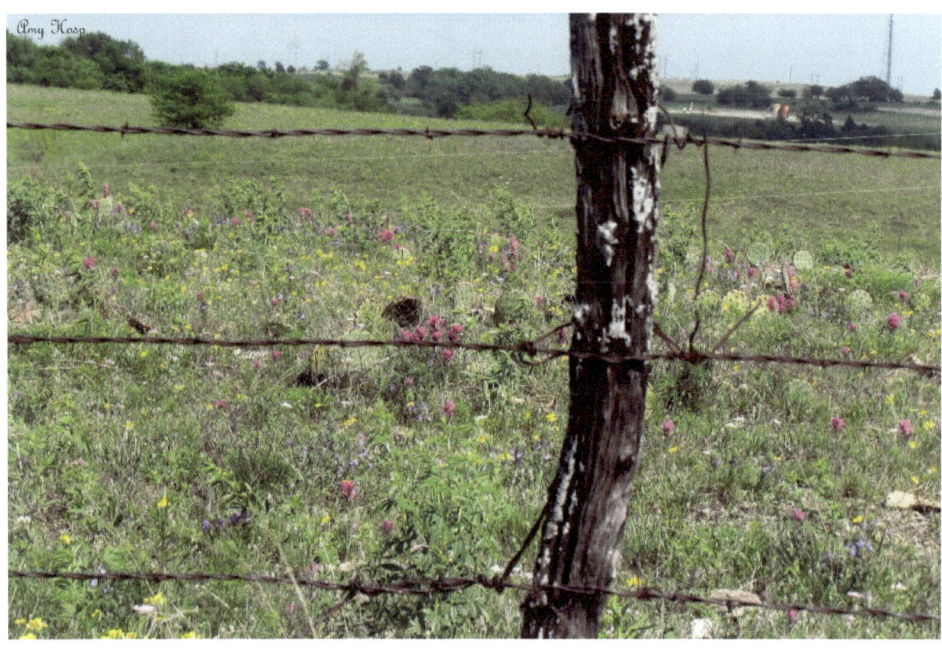

If I could brush a canvas with these pink beauties,
I would be considered a skilled colorist indeed.

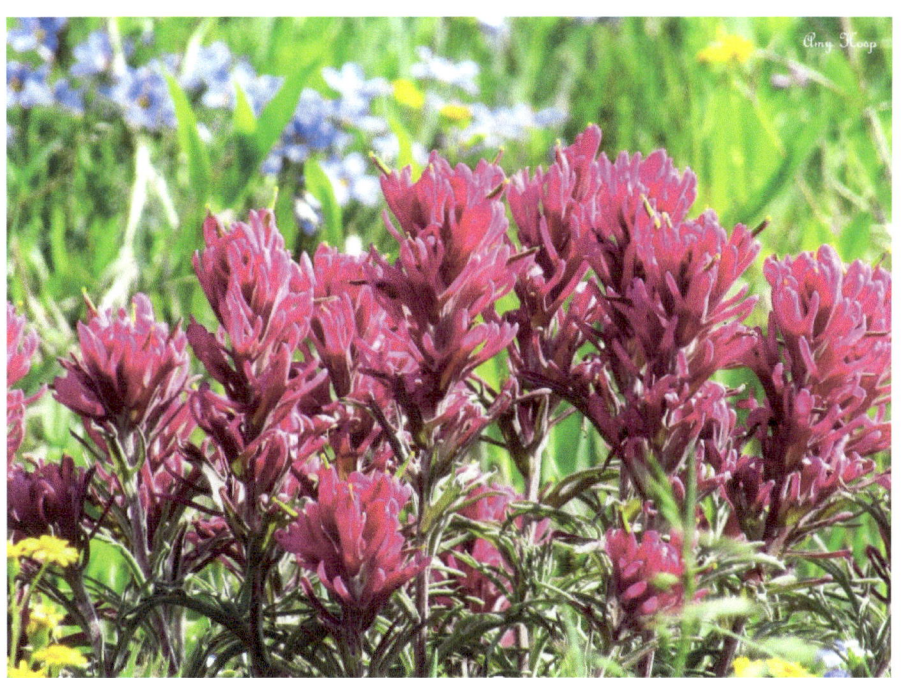

A meadow of peaceful softly flowing yellow beauties sprinkled with just the right amount of color is like looking at a glittery dream.

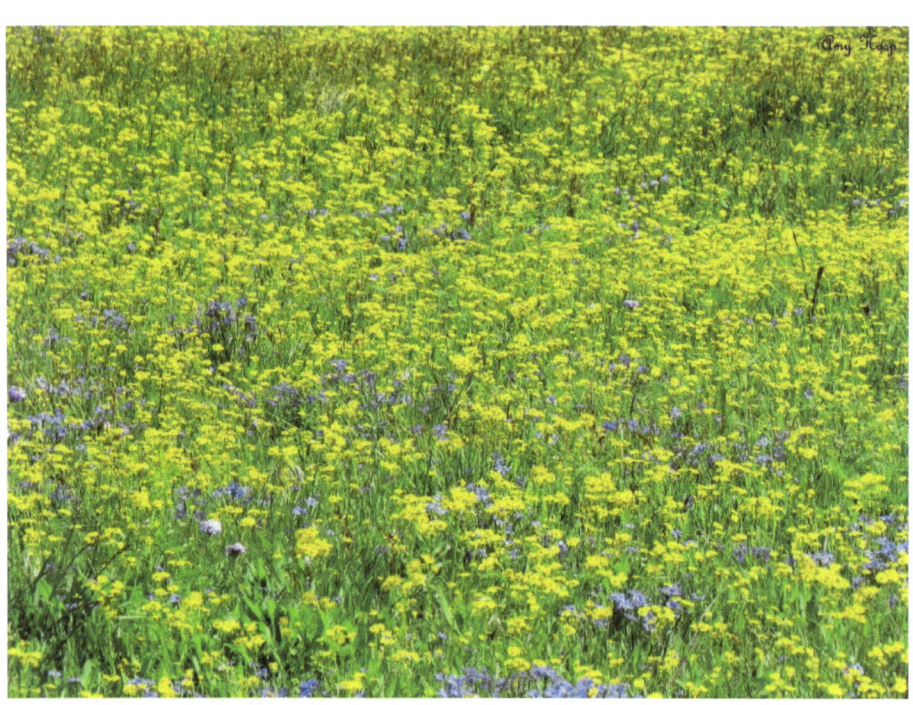

I wonder how many eyes have passed over this
meadow without seeing the flowers
much less their beauty.

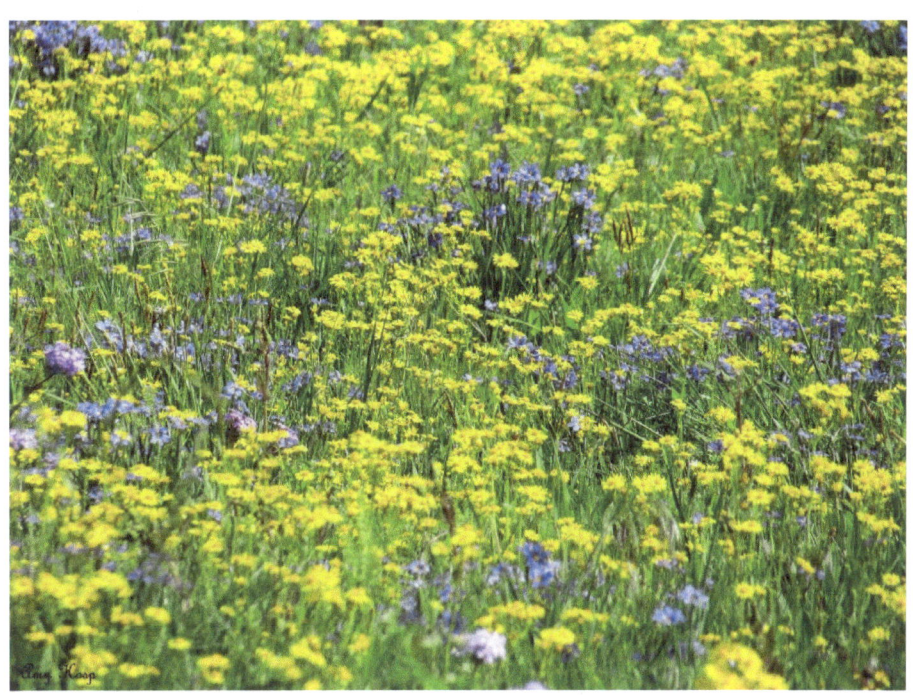

This bouquet of flowers reminds me of an Irish Proverb that says, "Tis better to buy a small bouquet and give to your friend this very day, then a bushel of roses white and red to lay on his coffin after he's dead."

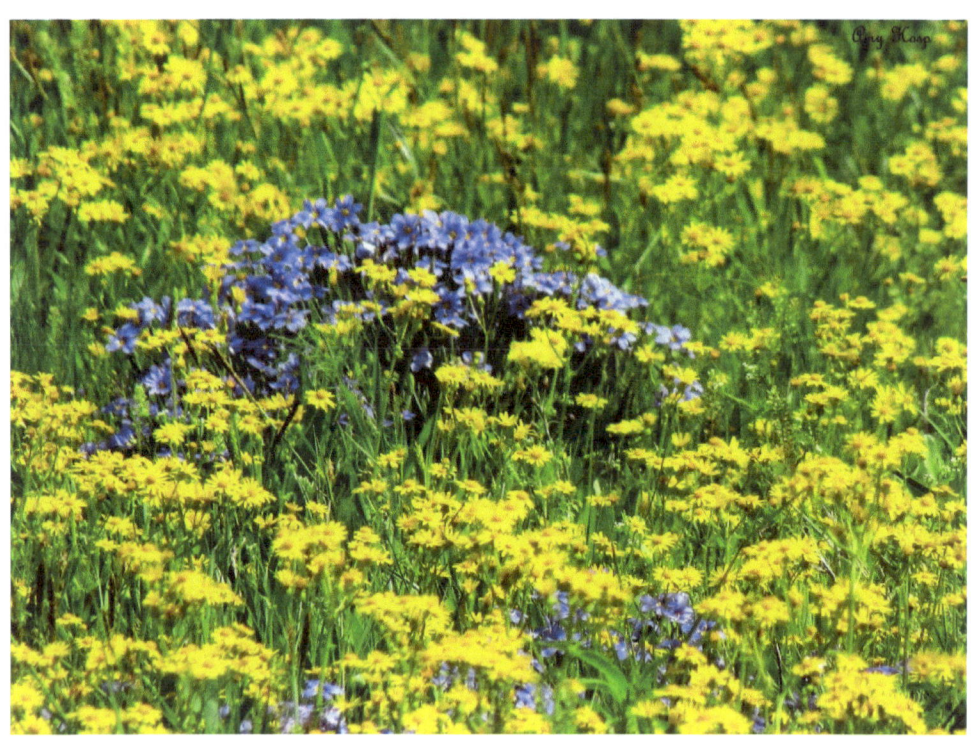

Verbena Lollipops sounds like such an old name but what a beautiful old name it is when it looks as beautiful and bright as these do.

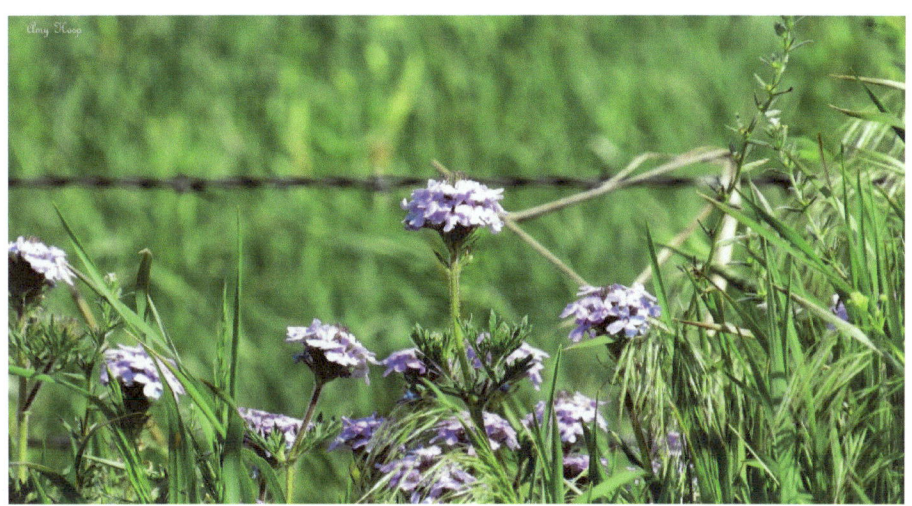

It's so pleasing to look at all the different types of flowers. They all look like they are showing off to us the creativity of God.

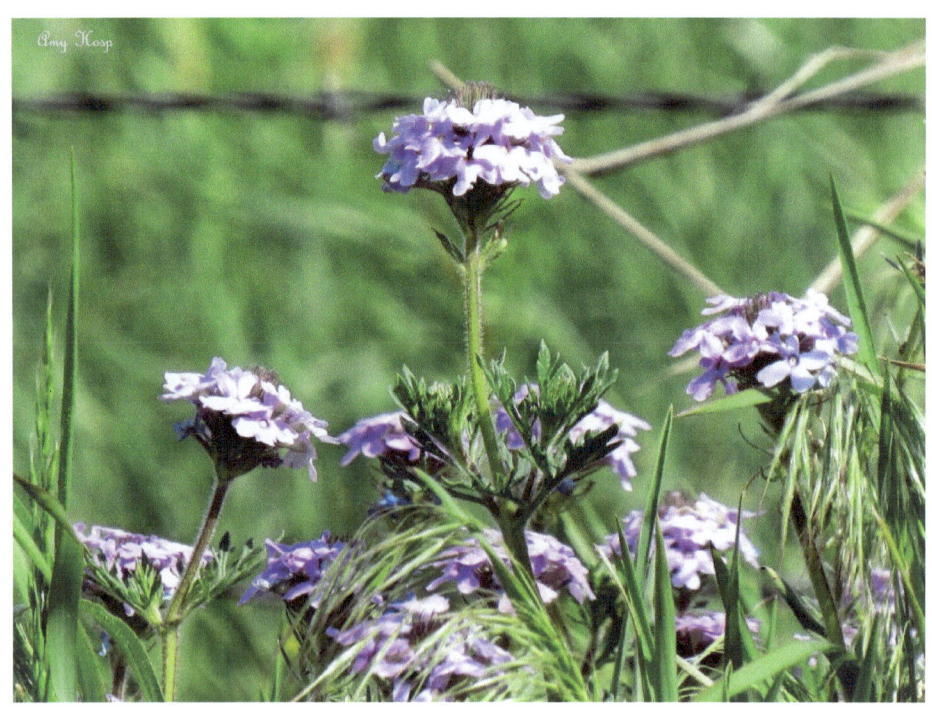

If I stop and listen very carefully, I can imagine that I hear these purple groups singing like a church choir sings the invitation to choose Jesus.

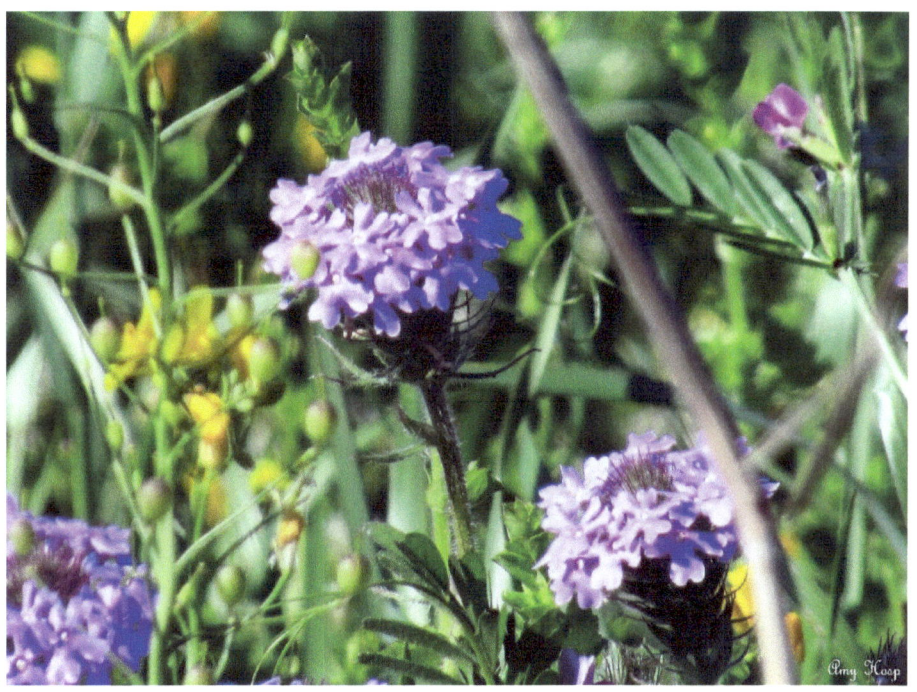

Beauty stands out among the hardness
if you just look for it.

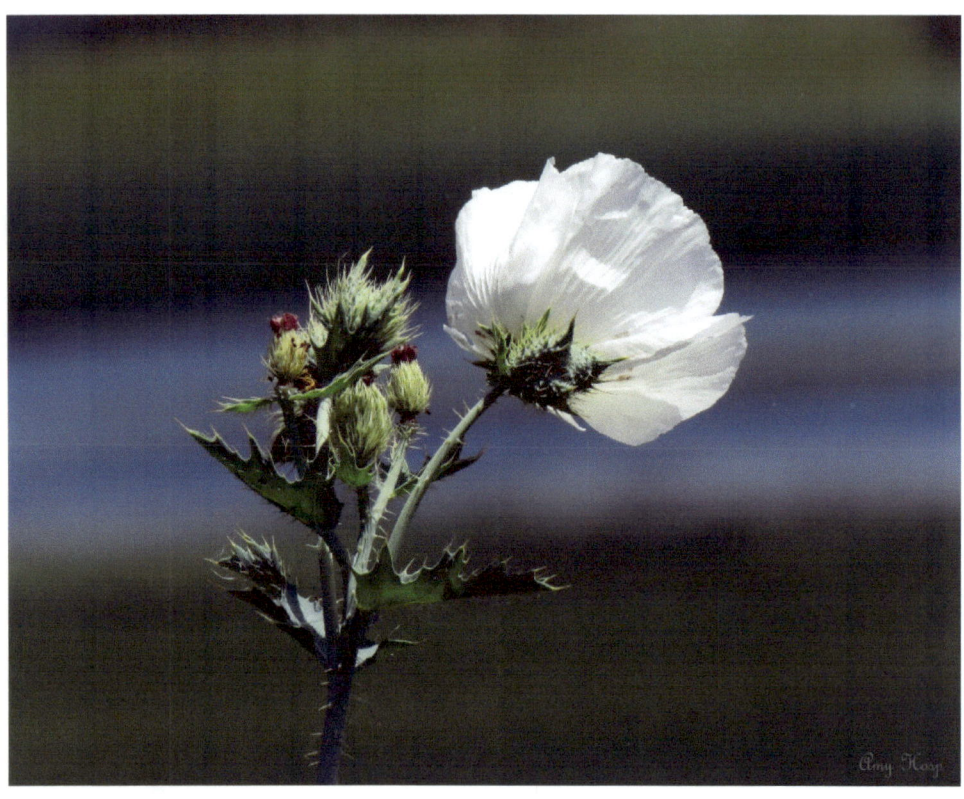

God gives us all that we need when we
feel like we are trapped in sticky places.

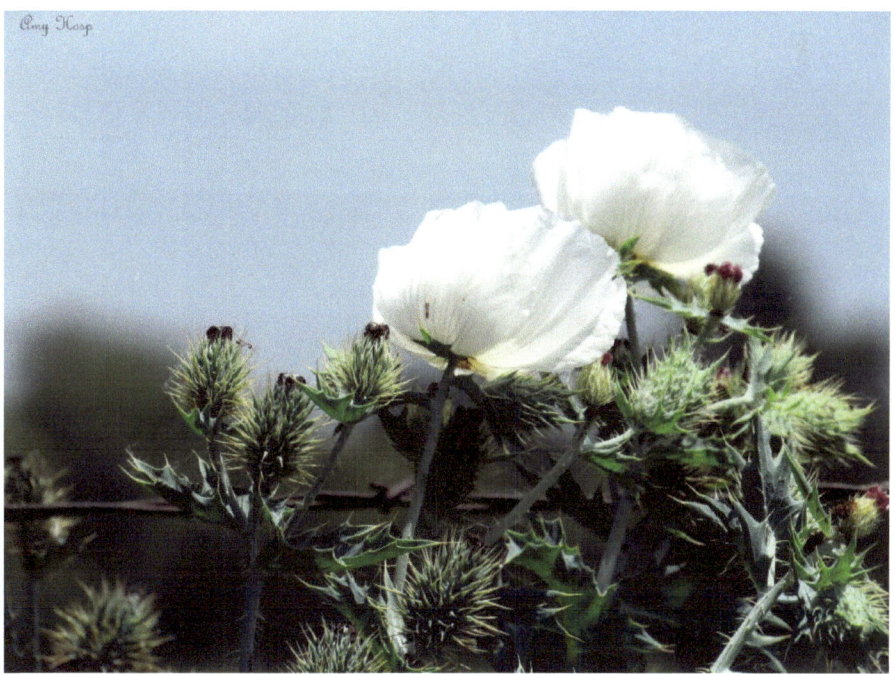

At times it's the dainty ones that make the biggest show.

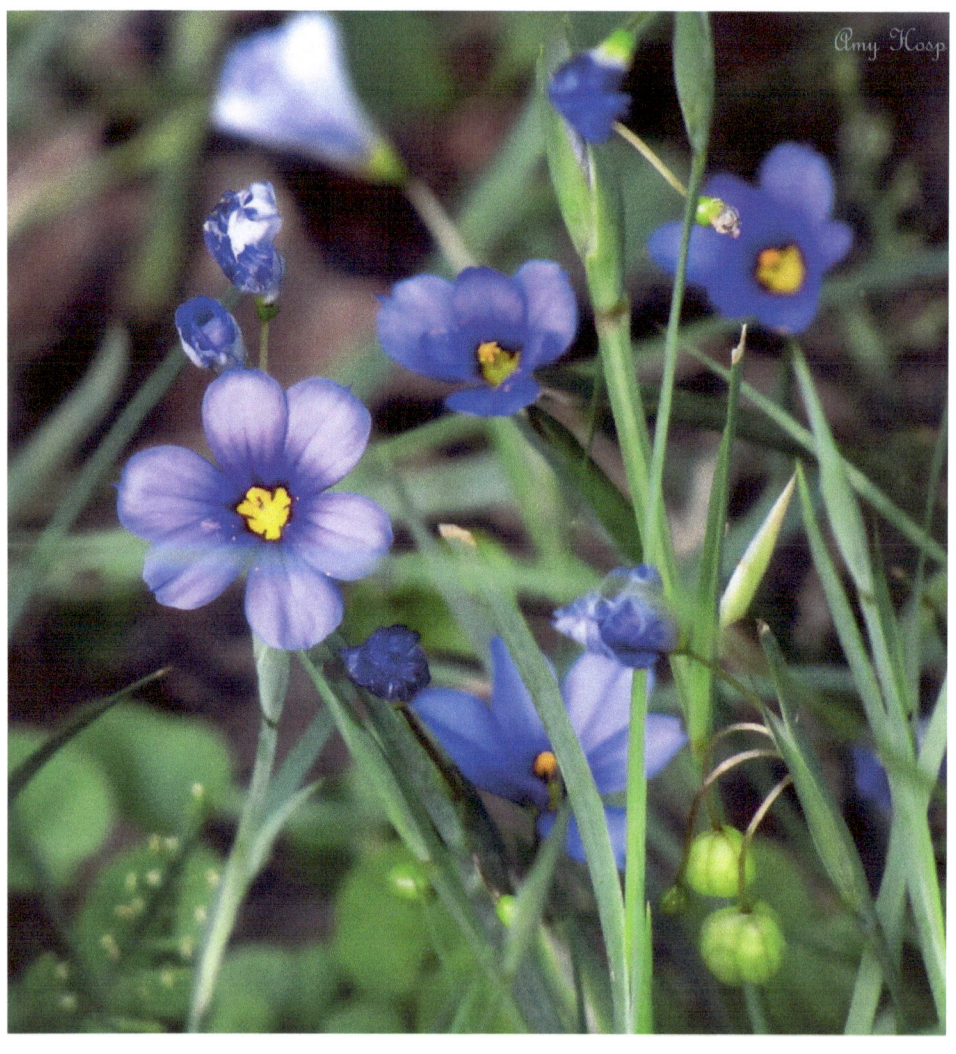

Honey Suckles always bring to me the best childhood memoires of a special lady who showed me how to harvest the sweet liquid of these beauties.

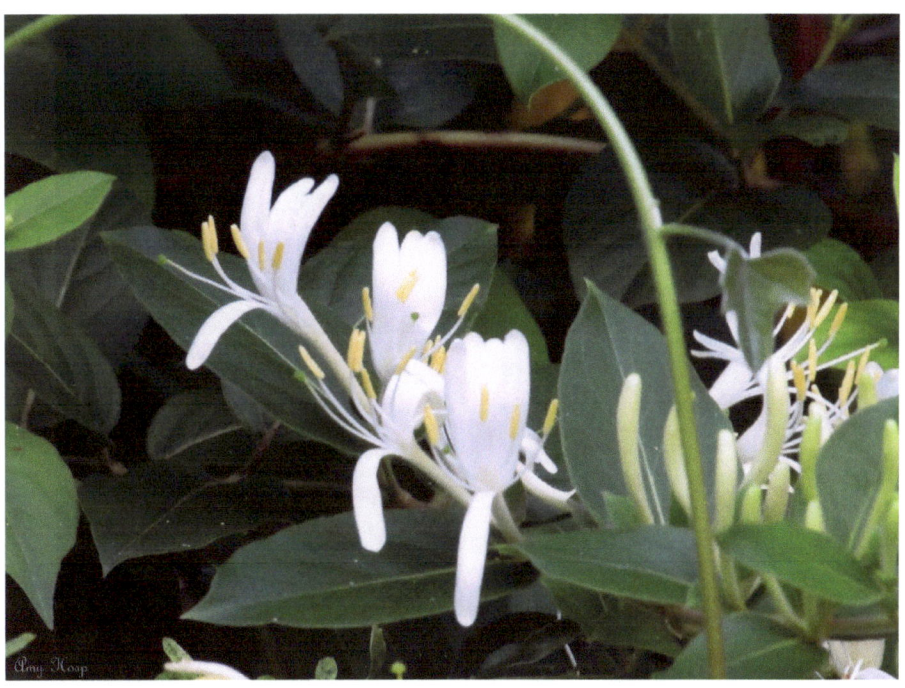

Sweetness comes in all shapes and sizes.

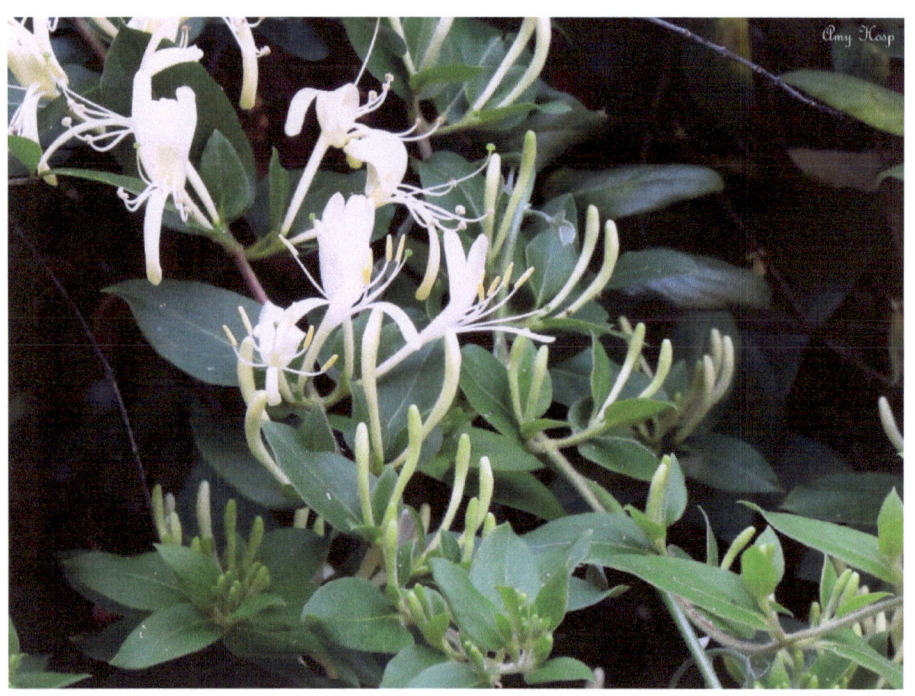

The beauty of the colors emerging in and out of each other is a perfect harmony which is a pansy.

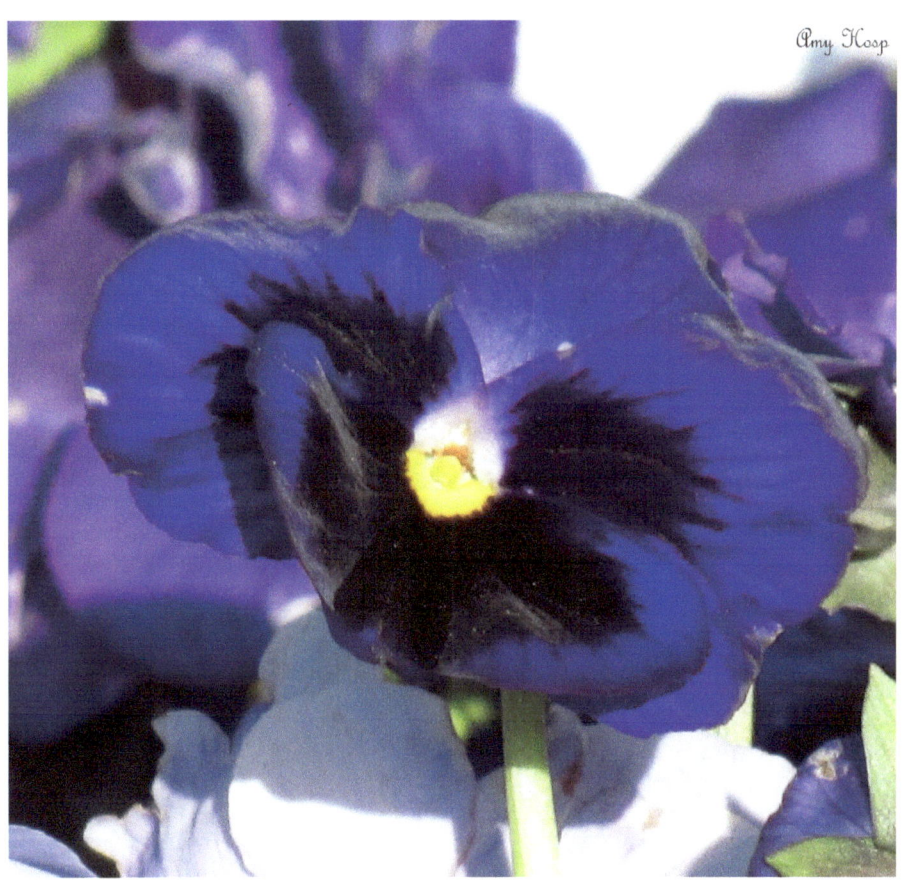

If Unicorns are real, their best friend is a flower.

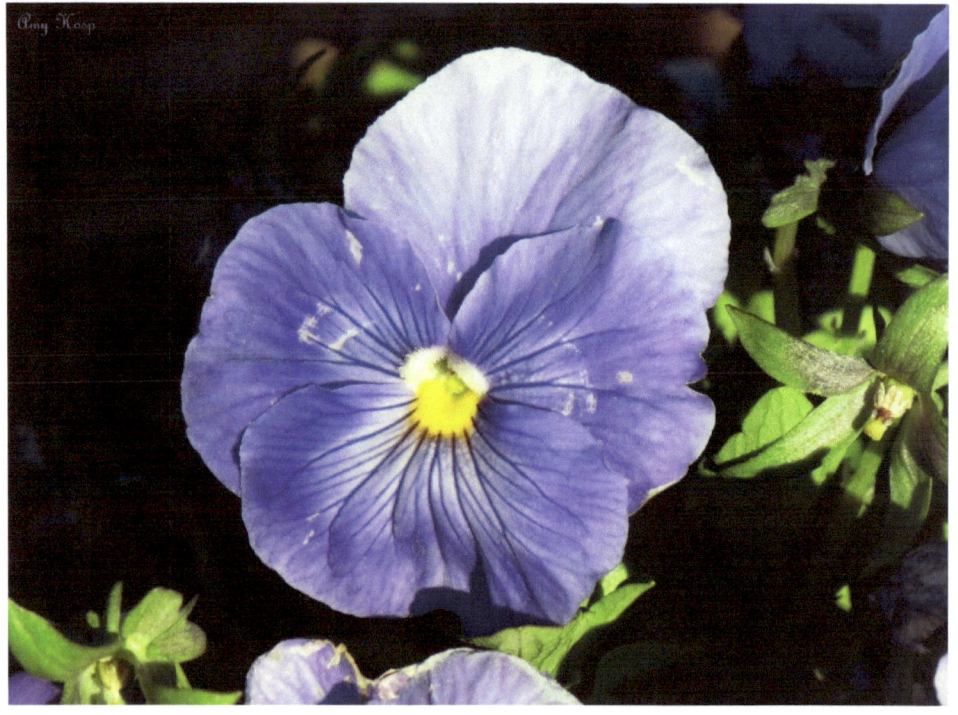

The pansy is symbolic of thought, clarity and reflecting upon our inner selves.

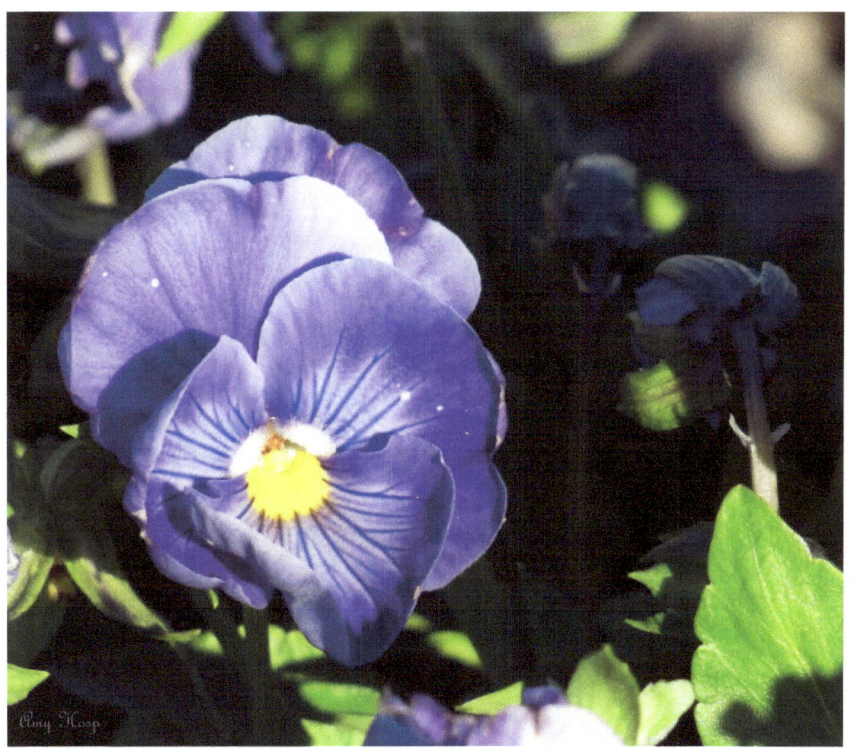

Flowers of all kinds shimmer in a special way when the due settles on them.

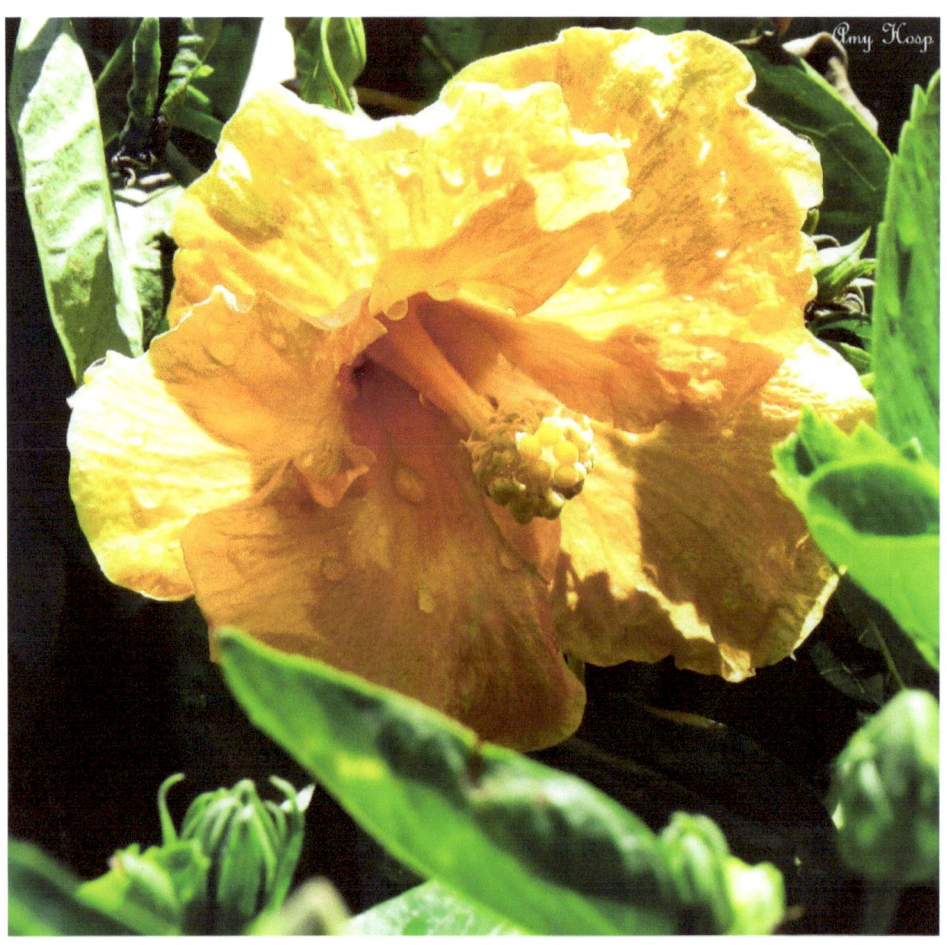

When you see into the center of a flower it opens
your heart to knowing that beauty
begins in the heart.

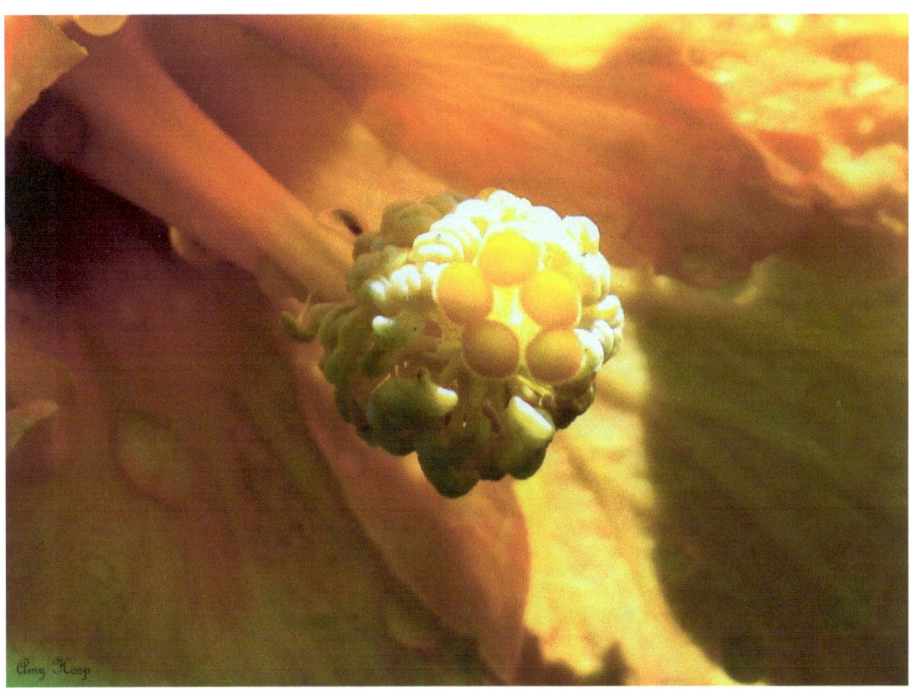

Even perfection hides itself at times.

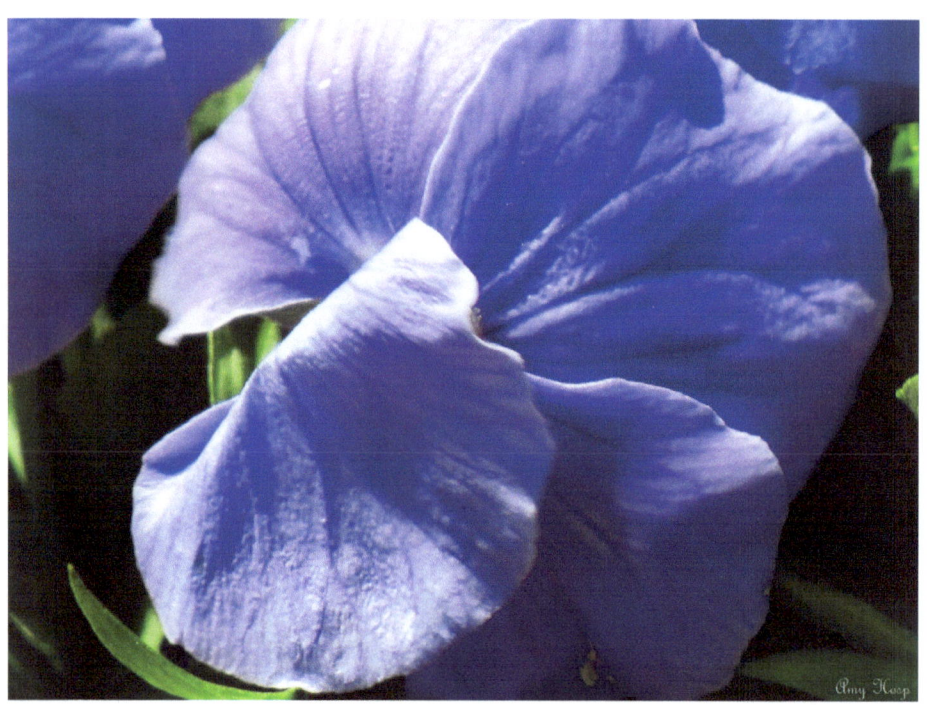

Flowers are an everlasting beauty of brightness that shins into the darkness.

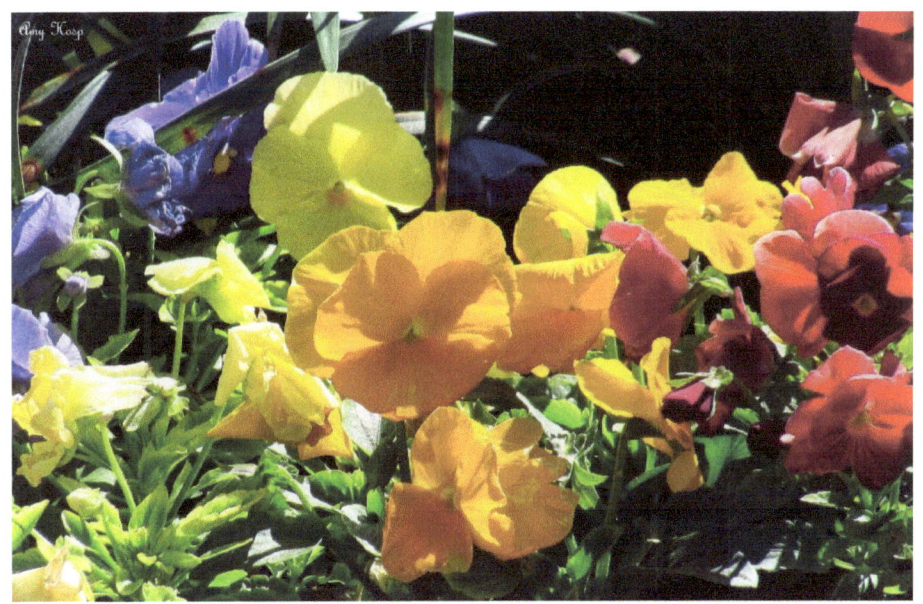

The yellow softness of these flowers reminds me of lemon pie.

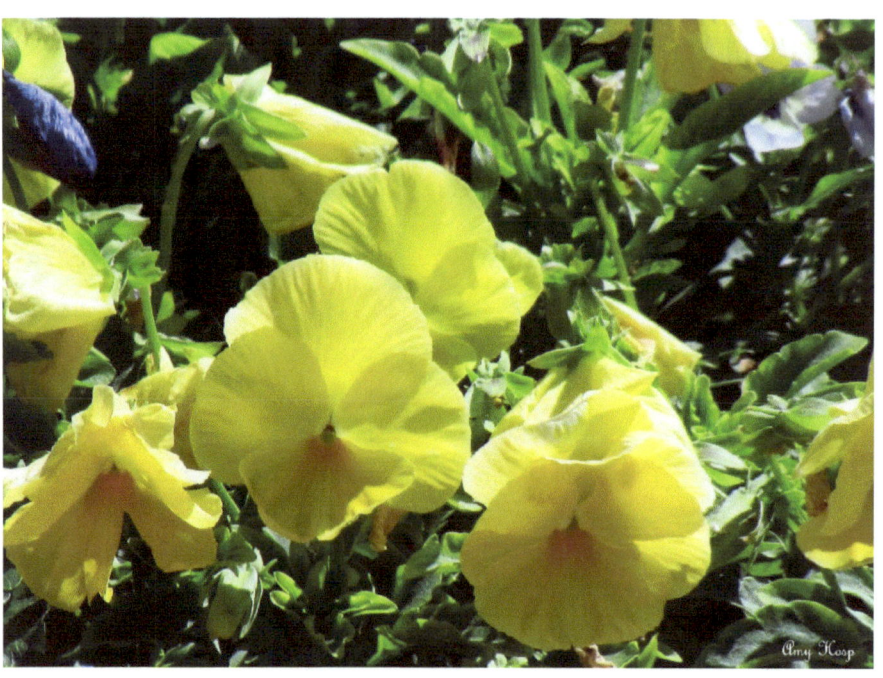

Flowers and sun go hand and hand.

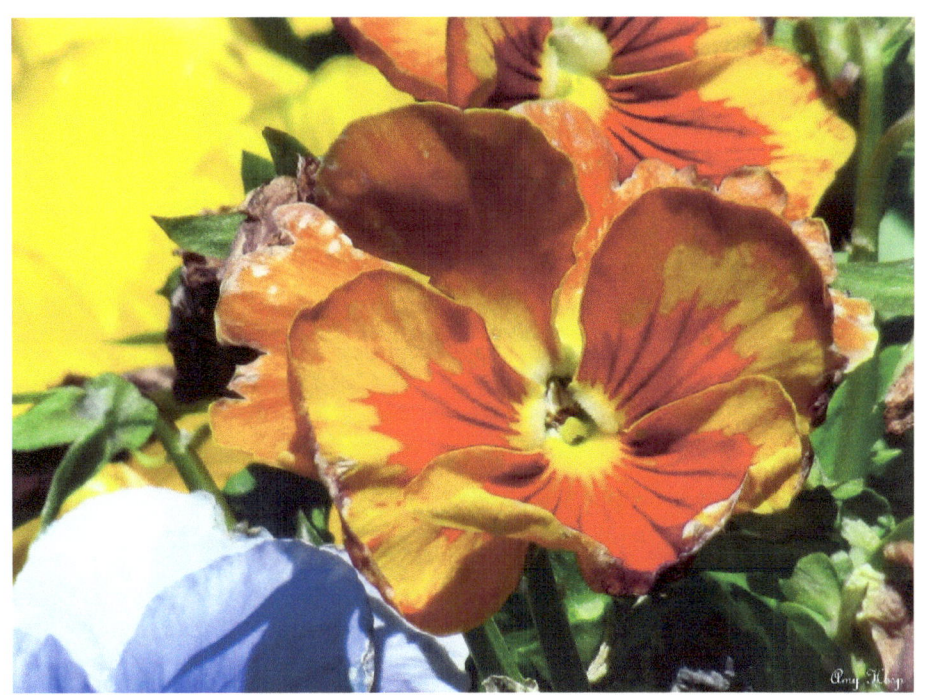

Flowers speak out inviting us
to come and enjoy their being.

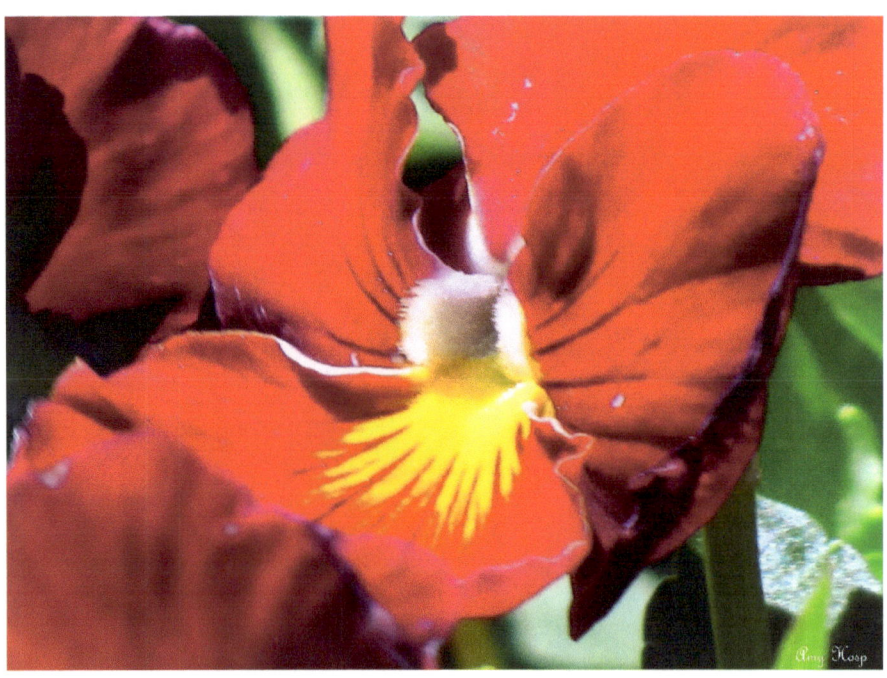

Flowers add living to our lives without
us even knowing they are doing it.

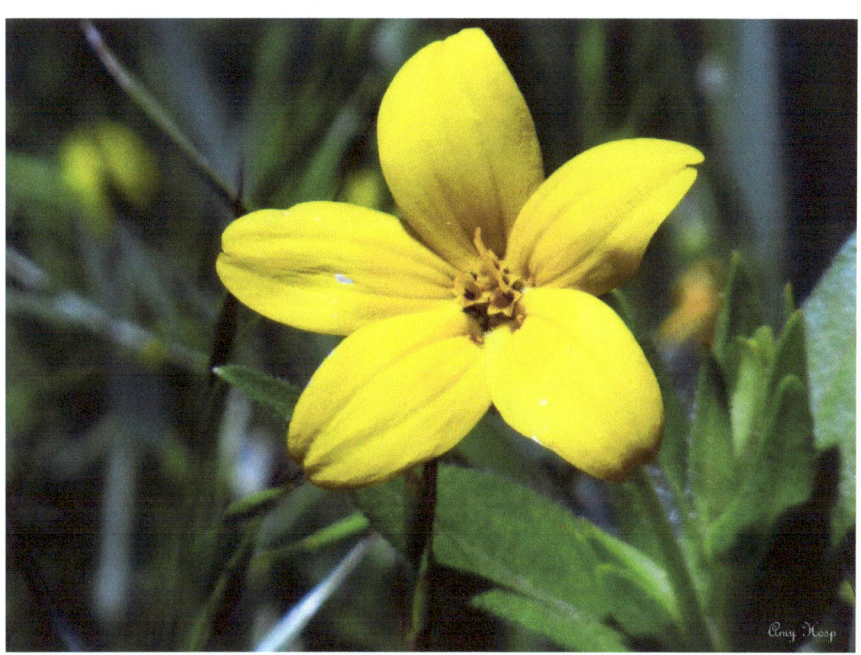

In the beginning things might look strange to some but it's all part of God's plan making creation into what He designed it to be.

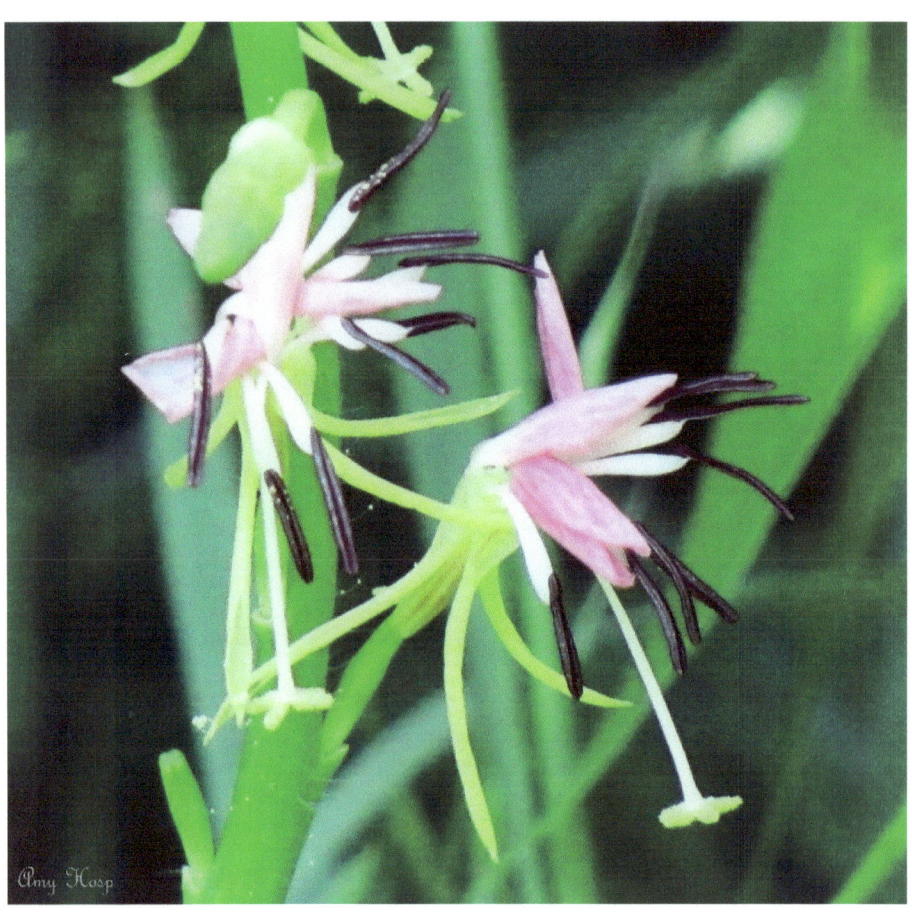

Flowers are beautiful in their own way
Just like a sloppy kiss on the check
from your favorite puppy.

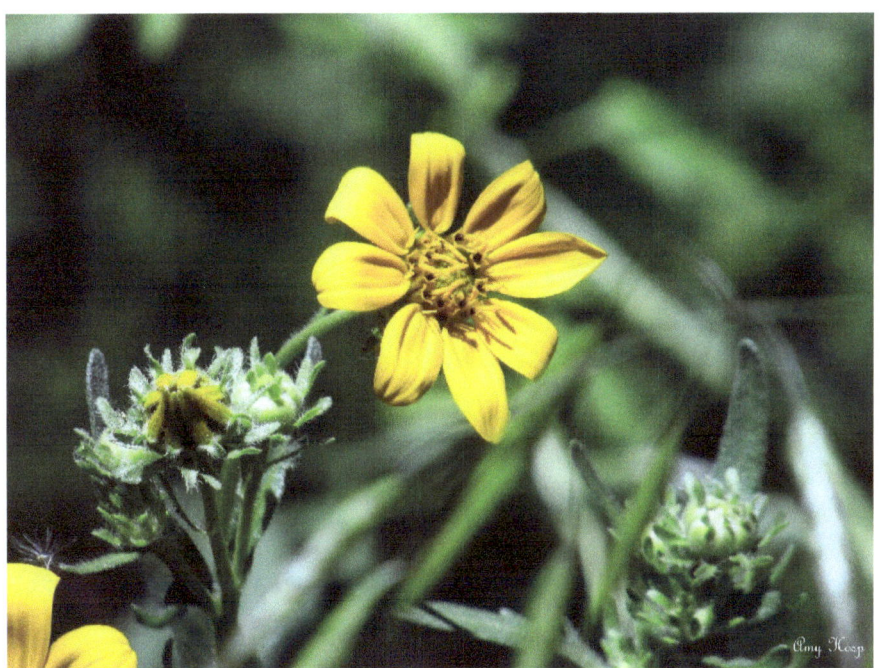

These beauties look like icing on a cake.

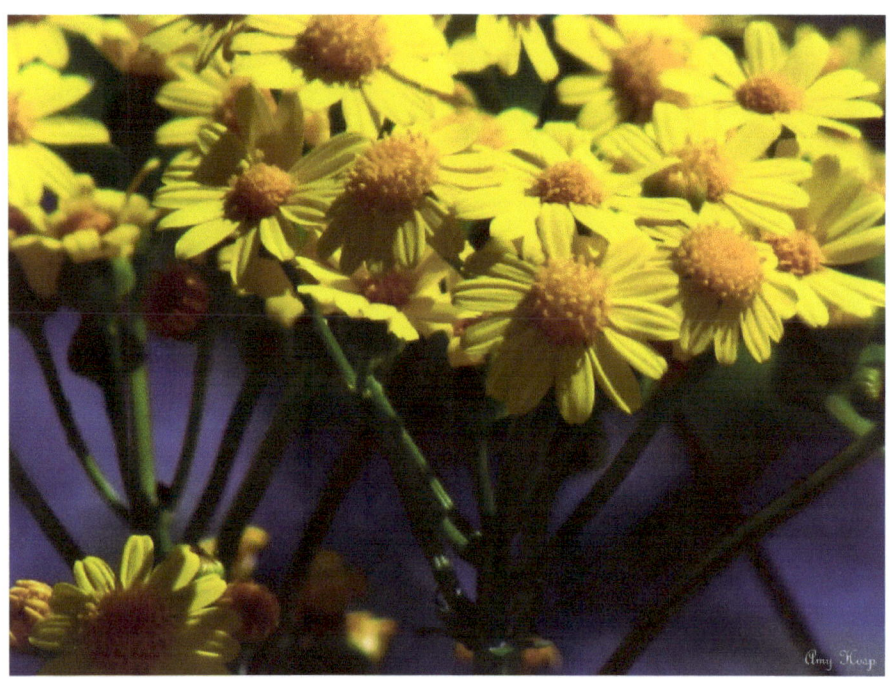

These False Purple Thistles are rare eye catching
stickers that look stunning in the sunlight.
They remind me that sometimes we have
to face the risk of pain
to touch the beauty.

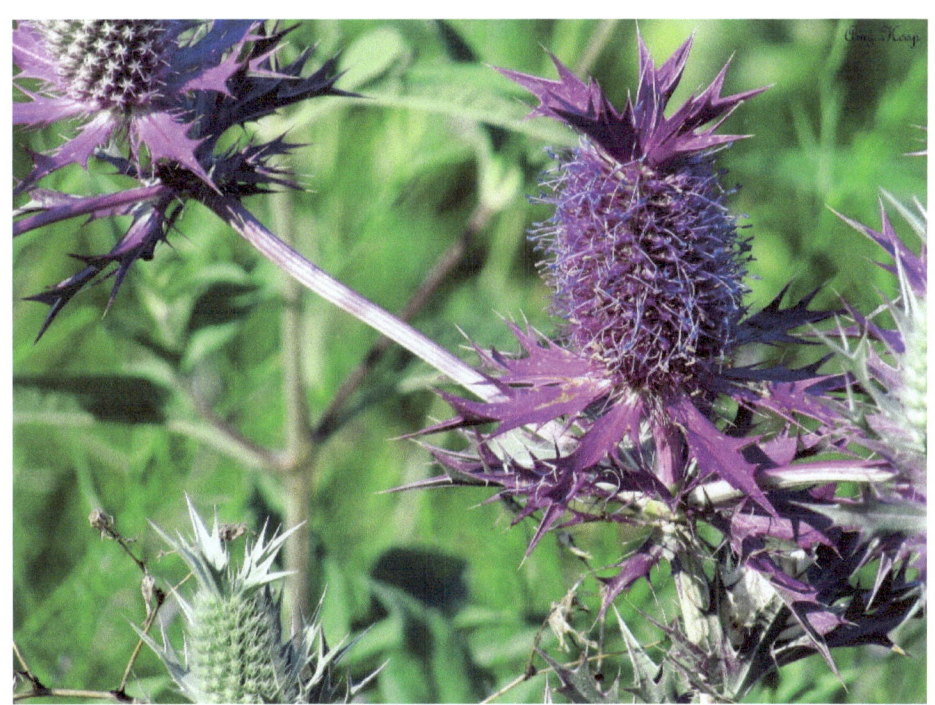

Even this wild weed reaches out to
us with its beauty.

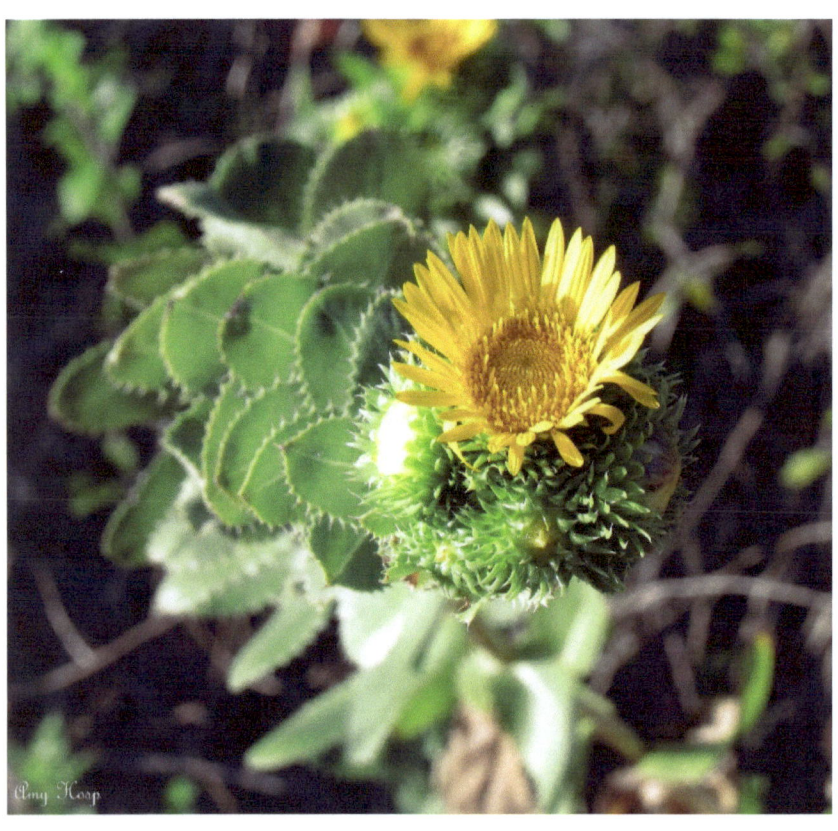

If all trumpets were this interesting
all music would sound sweeter.

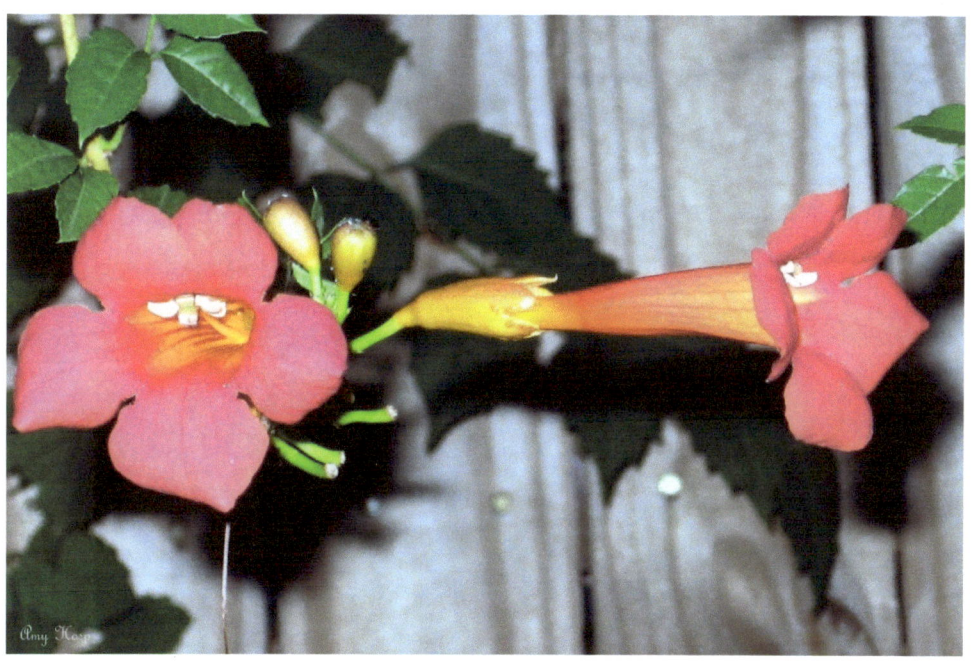

The magnolia is the sweetest smelling of all flowers.

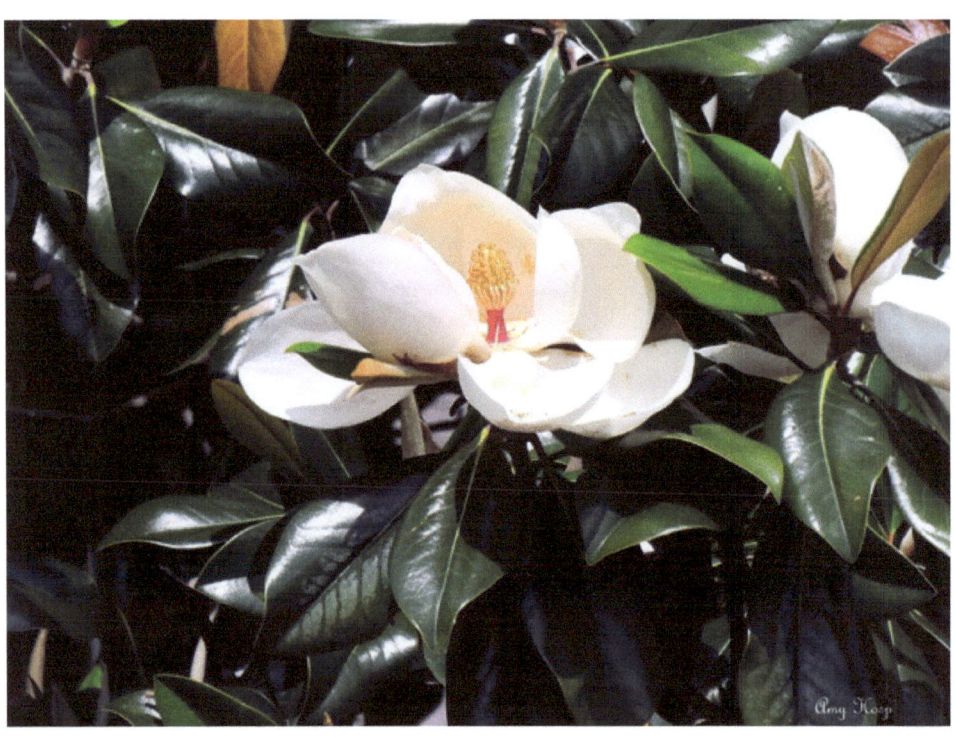

Standing up and out in a crowd is a great feature of the magnolia.

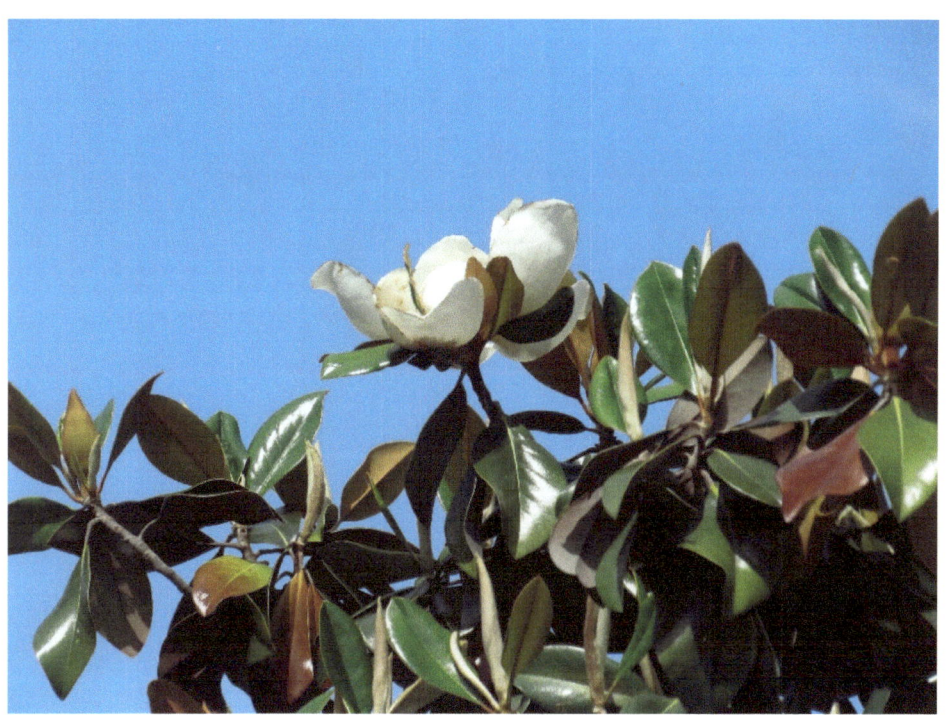

When Helen Keller said that love is like a beautiful flower, one that she might not touch but whose fragrance makes a garden a place of delight just the same, was speaking such profound truth!

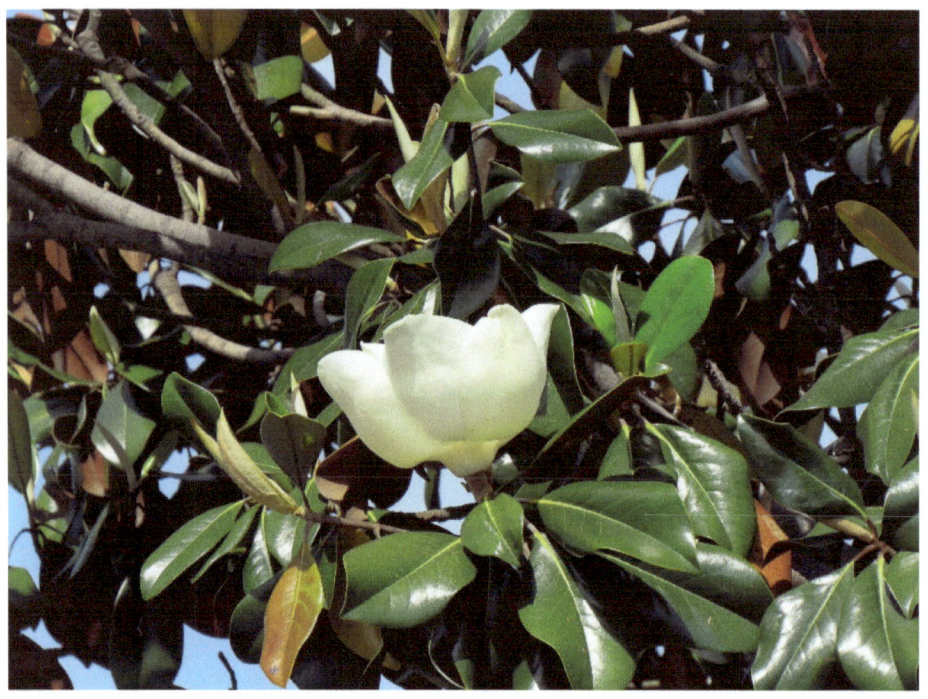

Find me at:

Education info about Ehlers Danlos Syndrome can be found at Genes That Don't Fit:
https://genesthatdontfit.net

Amy's Blogs:
www.thelibertyofitall.com

Amy's Photography:
https://amy-hosp.pixels.com

Amy's T-shirt store, The Liberty Of It All T-shirt Store:
https://teespring.com/stores/the-liberty-of-it-all

Liberty's Instagram page:
https://www.instagram.com/liberty_the_ehlers_danlos_dog

Liberty's Facebook page:
https://www.facebook.com/LibertyEDSdog

Liberty's Book, Ehlers Danlos Syndrome with Liberty The Dog:
https://www.amazon.com/dp/1723438138

I love adventure and capturing the uniqueness of each adventure, whether at home or out on the road! I love to take the unknown road and see where it takes me. It is on trips like these where I have learned to see the unusual, the old, the new, the beauty and the familiarness of my beloved state, Texas. Most of my photos are taken from my car, yes, you heard me right, they are taken from my car window or from the moon roof because I have a few rare genetic disorders which makes it hard for me to get out of my car and walk around. I hope that you enjoy my quirky photos and art and that you are inspired to go out and see what all is picture-worthy in your life.

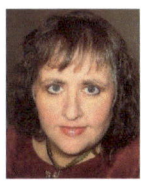

About the Author:

Amy Hosp grew up in Frisco TX and she is a graduate of Dallas Christian College where she earned a B.S. in Ministry & Leadership and has spent some time working toward earning a master's degree at Southwestern Baptist Theological Seminary in Ft. Worth TX. In 2005 Amy served as a missionary in Nigeria. In 2012 Amy was diagnosed with a rare genetic disorder called Ehlers Danlos Syndrome Classical Type I and in 2018 another rare genetic disorder call Osteogenesis Imperfecta Type I. This extremely rare combination of genetic disorders causes a host of health issues that has left Amy disabled. Despite her disabilities Amy enjoys random adventures ranging from a spur of the moment road trip to the country, to exploring ideas of the unknown in life. Her life is a voyage and she wants to invite you to go along with her and find in you, what she has and is still finding, "The person that God created me to be!"

Amy is a writer, photographer, musician and a missionary. She deals with life by always looking for the positive side to every situation and she will leave you with a smile. Her passion is to challenge the minds of others to look deep inside of themselves and look at life from a different perspective and to find the true gifting's of God in their lives. Amy brings a unique view to understanding God's fullness and happiness for today's Christian believer.

www.ingramcontent.com/pod-product-compliance
Lightning Source LLC
Chambersburg PA
CBHW040233220526
45473CB00001B/221